# MARCO 🌐 POLO

Tips

# CANADA WEST

## ROCKY MOUNTAINS, VANCOUVER

Arctic Ocean

Polar circle

Alaska
(USA)

Nunavut

Yukon    Northern
         Canada
PACIFIC   **CANADA**
OCEAN       West

British
Columbia              Manitoba

Alberta               Ontario

Vancouver    Saskatchewan

USA

The best Insider Tips → p. 4

INSIDER TIP

Vancouver → p. 32

Vancouver Island → p. 40

British Columbia → p. 50

**SYMBOLS**

| INSIDER TIP | Insider Tip |
| ★ | Highlight |
| ●●●● | Best of ... |
| ☒ | Scenic view |
| ☺ | Responsible travel: fair trade principles and the environment respected |
| (*) | Telephone numbers that are not toll-free |

**PRICE CATEGORIES HOTELS**

*Expensive*   over C$200

*Moderate*   C$110–C$200

*Budget*   under C$110

The prices are per double room without breakfast. Single rooms are seldom cheaper

**PRICE CATEGORIES RESTAURANTS**

*Expensive*   over C$35

*Moderate*   C$20–C$35

*Budget*   under C$20

The prices are valid for a main course dinner incl. tax. At lunchtime it is about 40–50 per cent cheaper

On the cover: West Coast Trail – spectacular wilderness p. 103 | Vineyards, lakes & beaches p. 58

# CONTENTS

Rocky Mountains → p. 66

Alberta → p. 80

Northern Canada → p. 90

Road atlas → p. 124

INSIDE BACK COVER: PULL-OUT MAP →

## DID YOU KNOW?

## MAPS IN THE GUIDEBOOK

(126 A1) Page numbers and coordinates refer to the road atlas
(0) Site/address located off the map. Coordinates are also given for places that are not marked on the road atlas
(U A1) Coordinates refer to the street map of Vancouver inside the back cover

## PULL-OUT MAP

(𝄞 A–B 2–3) Refers to the removable pull-out map
(𝄞 a–b 2–3) Refers to the additional inset maps on the pull-out map

# The best MARCO POLO Insider Tips

## Our top 15 Insider Tips

INSIDER TIP **On a bear hunt – with a camera**

With a little luck you will be able to see some of the resident black bears up close from the boat (photo above) in the bays around Tofino. In the summer the bear mothers here teach their cubs how to crack mussels → **p. 45**

INSIDER TIP **Starfish ahoy!**

Seemingly weightless floating jellyfish, colourful sea anemones, giant octopus , starfish, wolf eels and and many other marine animals live in the Shaw Ocean Discovery Centre north of Victoria – but only for a while, then they are returned to the sea → **p. 49**

INSIDER TIP **Picture-perfect town**

The historic trading post of Fort Langley, on the Fraser River, has often been the backdrop for Hollywood movies – with a little luck you might cross paths with a star who is filming a movie there → **p. 39**

INSIDER TIP **Visit the culinary world of Asia**

Strange spices, durian fruit, live crabs and duck feet: the T & T Supermarket on the edge of the Chinatown in Vancouver offers all the gourmet treasures of Asia → **p. 35**

INSIDER TIP **A river full of salmon**

In early October the Adams River, north-east of Kamloops, swarms with hundreds of thousands of bright red salmon → **p. 56**

INSIDER TIP **Log cabins on the lake**

Thick beams, red roofs and breathtaking vistas: the Clearwater Lake Lodge off Hwy. 20 meets all the requirements for a wilderness adventure → **p. 53**

INSIDER TIP **Hot springs in the wilderness**

Pure relaxation after a long walk: soak sore muscles in the Nakusp Hot Springs pools, wonderfully secluded in the woods → **p. 58**

**INSIDER TIP** Crazy Canadians
A race with decorated toilets on wheels? The Klondike International Outhouse Race proves that nothing is too crazy for the gold miners in Dawson City → **p. 113**

**INSIDER TIP** Good wine, beautiful view
Quail's Gate Estate Winery on the shore of Okanagan Lake in the wine area of Kelowna offers the perfect gourmet lunch → **p. 60**

**INSIDER TIP** Canoe trip just like the early pioneers
A multi-day canoe trip on the lakes of the Wells Gray Provincial Park opens the eyes and the heart – and also gives you calluses on your hands! → **p. 62**

**INSIDER TIP** Original cowboy boots
Here you will certainly be spoilt for choice, the Alberta Boot Company in Calgary has 12,000 boots in stock – or you can order a custom pair → **p. 83**

**INSIDER TIP** A night in a house of pleasure
Bombay Peggy's in Dawson City (photo below) really was once a brothel – today it is a B & B with a good pub → **p. 92**

**INSIDER TIP** A hike with scenic views
In good weather Parker Ridge has the most beautiful views of the Rockies and the mighty glaciers which flow into the three lakes from here → **p. 99**

**INSIDER TIP** Rustic pioneer lodge
You will feel as if you have been transported back to the Wild West in the Num-Ti-Jah Lodge in Banff National Park → **p. 70**

**INSIDER TIP** Adventurous spelunking
Be an intrepid cave explorer: the caverns and crystal formations of the Horne Lake Caves Provincial Park on Vancouver Island are still in their original state → **p. 110**

# BEST OF ...

**FOR FREE**

● *Salmon viewing in Vancouver*

Instead of going to an aquarium, you can see wild salmon up close and for free at the *Capilano Salmon Hatchery* in the summer. Watch the fish fight against the flow through large underwater observation windows → p. 34

● *Gold rush town*

Historic *Dawson City* could almost be a museum village, but the authentic gold rush town established in 1898 is alive and kicking and offers wonderful photo opportunities and plenty pioneer flair (photo) without any entrance fee → p. 91

● *Sunny mountains, dizzying heights*

National parks charge admission but provincial parks in Alberta, such as *Kananaskis Country* are free. The of the Rocky Mountains here are just as beautiful as in Banff – but much sunnier, because it is the eastern flank of the mountains → p. 75

● *Olympic musical moments*

Today free concerts take place where gold medals were handed out in 1988. In the summer musicians perform on the *Olympic Plaza* in Calgary – and there are always new festivals that invite you to celebrate → p. 81

● *Enjoyment of art for free*

'Art for all' is the motto of the *Vancouver Art Gallery* every Tuesday evening, when admission is free. Those who want to can leave a donation. Worth seeing: Emily Carr's impressionistic and expansive paintings of the rugged west coast → p. 38

● *Cliff hiking*

Landscaped and paved trails are few and far between on the west coast – and they usually cost money such as in the Pacific Rim National Park. The *Wild Pacific Trail* right next door in Ucluelet is free and truly stunning. Start with the Lighthouse Loop section! → p. 45

●●●● Dots in guidebook refer to 'Best of ...' tips

● *Celebrate with lumberjacks*

It doesn't get more Canadian than the *Salmon Festival* in Campbell River on Vancouver Island where salmon and lumberjacks are celebrated – with axe throwing and bowsaw competitions → p. 113

● *Across the Arctic Circle*

The trip on Canada's northernmost road takes two days: the 700km/435mi *Dempster Highway* runs through the wilderness from Dawson City across the Arctic Circle through the Mackenzie Delta → p. 93

● *Orca watching*

It is a strict rule that no one is allowed to get closer than 100m/300ft from the whales. But the inquisitive creatures often come closer to the boats and you may experience this on a whale watching tour in Victoria with *Orca Spirit Adventures* → p. 48

● *Smoked salmon in Vancouver*

At the Granville Island *Public Market* in Vancouver you can sample the culinary treasures of Canada's west coast: raspberries, goat's cheese, oysters, halibut – and the best smoked salmon in the world. Try some Indian Candy → p. 35

● *Trapper for a day*

How about spending the night as a fur trapper? Deep in the wilderness of British Columbia the wooden stockades and beaver pelts of the *Fort St. James National Historic Site* take you back to the era of the fur trader → p. 64

● *Cycling around Stanley Park*

On a sunny afternoon, there is no better outing in Vancouver than the more than 10km/6mi long *Stanley Park Drive*. The route winds its way along the coast with great views of the city, the mountains, the fjords and small beaches → p. 36

● *Lake views in the Rocky Mountains*

The view from *Bow Summit Pass* – 2000m/6560ft and sometimes windy – over Peyto Lake is quite stunning. The strikingly turquoise glacial lake is one of the most impressive sights in the Rockies (photo) → p. 69

ONLY IN

# BEST OF ...

● *Outlet shopping in Calgary*
Shopping is cheap (and you will stay dry) in *Crossiron Mills* in Calgary, the largest indoor discount mall in Canada. Some 200 shops offer from everything from stilettos to Stetsons → p. 83

● *Dinosaurs in Drumheller*
Alberta's badlands experience intense thunderstorms with pouring rain and if you get caught in one then take refuge in Drumheller's *Royal Tyrrell Museum* (photo). The bonus: when it rains, the fossil beds are laid bare – perhaps you will discover a new type of dinosaur → p. 85

● *Underwater in the Vancouver Aquarium*
While away a rainy day in the large, well designed *Vancouver Aquarium*, where beluga whales can be observed in the underwater Arctic viewing area → p. 36

● *A rainforest in the rain*
Rainforests flourish on the west coast of Vancouver Island, such as in the *Pacific Rim National Park*. Naturally it rains here often. Whales and bears are not disturbed by the rain – and hopefully neither will you be → p. 44

● *Take a ferry ride up the coast*
Dark pine forests, blue fjords, leaping orca: on a trip through the *Inside Passage* can you sit high and dry and let the mystical, misty fjord world pass you by → p. 46

● *Drown your sorrows in the Ranchman's Saloon*
Your bad weather blues will disappear with beer, tasty ribs and country songs in the *Ranchman's Saloon* in Calgary. When it rains you have an even greater chance of meeting some real cowboys – they knock off work earlier then → p. 84

RAIN

**CHILL OUT**

● *View the Rockies from a boat*
Why hike if the view from the water is even more beautiful? The half day *Waterton Shoreline Cruise* (in a historic little boat) shows the southern Rockies in Canada from their best side – and you can even make a whistle-stop visit over the border into the United States → **p. 77**

● *A spa on a ranch*
After the ride enjoy a relaxing massage – the *Echo Valley Ranch* in the BC heartland offers a real Thai spa with soothing treatments, massages, herbal baths and yoga classes. Worth seeing: the original Thai bathhouse → **p. 56**

● *Drinking wine in the Okanagan Valley*
The sunny slopes along the lakes of Okanagan Valley have some of the Canada's best vineyards. Why not see for yourself with a wine tasting on the terrace of the *Mission Hill Winery* at Kelowna → **p. 59**

● *Relax in hot springs*
Nothing could be better on a wet, cold day than to relax in some hot mineral water. The *Radium Hot Springs* are ideal for this, but there are also other places in the Rockies where you can quickly ease your aching muscles (photo) → **p. 72**

● *Dive into a crystal world*
A cold sauna? Yes, that is right, at an eye-watering –110°C/–116°F (very briefly) the skin and immune system are stimulated. The *Sparkling Hill* spa in Vernon also boasts a unique crystal décor incorporating 3.5 million Swarovski crystals → **p. 60**

● *Into the wilderness on the Yukon*
Another way to relax is to canoe on the Yukon River from Whitehorse to Dawson City. Slowly paddle and drift through the wilderness. Equipment and rental canoes are available at *Kanoe People* in Whitehorse → **p. 95**

INTRODUCTION

# DISCOVER WESTERN CANADA!

During the Winter Olympics in Vancouver 2010, western Canada charmed the world with its wild, rugged beauty. This is the ideal place for outdoor enthusiasts to live the dream, to watch a family of bears on the shores of a fjord, enjoy the silence of the mighty Yukon River, to camp with cowboys in the vastness of the prairies or to go rafting through wild river rapids.

Somehow people believe that they know Canada. It lies on the same latitude as central Europe, and the climate is not much different from that of Europe, the mountains resemble the Alps, the coasts resemble those of Norway. And yet, western Canada is completely different – huge, epic, impressive, lonely. It lacks people, the noisy motorways and urban sprawl, and occupied parcels of land and field. Instead there is an unending and vast expanse of nature and almost every hike up to a mountain

Photo: Fisgard lighthouse in Victoria

Western Canada – especially British Columbia – is one of the leading wood exporters

summit is rewarded with a panoramic view of a landscape without roads or houses. Here the breathtaking landscape is still unspoilt and pristine.

**Fjord coasts and mountains crowned with glaciers**

First of all, you will have to get used to Canada's dimensions. A trip to the next shop that could be situated 50km/30mi away is barely worth mentioning. The west of Canada, the provinces of Alberta and British Columbia, the Yukon and the Northwest Territories covers more than a million square miles. You could fit France and Germany into the province of British Columbia alone, which only has 4.6 million inhabitants.

For a first trip to Canada the western part, with its varied landscapes, is the ideal destination. On the Pacific coast – full of fjords – the glacier-crowned Coast Mountains rise up, with their ancient and mysterious rainforests, from the dark waters, the home of whales and king salmon. Behind the mountains lie sunny plateaus rich in forests and lakes – interspersed with mountain ranges – that extend out as far as the Rocky Mountains. The Rocky Mountains have the most beautiful national parks in the country,

**Around 35,000 BC**
Paleo-Indians migrate across the Bering Strait to North America

**1535/1536**
Frenchman Jacques Cartier discovers the St. Lawrence River and uses the name Canada

**1670**
Royal charter by King Charles II establishes the Hudson's Bay Company, granting a monopoly over the fur trade and incorporating the land in the drainage basin of Hudson Bay

**1763**
New France becomes a British colony; fur traders open up the west

Banff and Jasper, connected by the Icefields Parkway, a spectacular scenic road. Even further eastwards, beyond the Rockies, is the ranch country of Alberta, where dinosaurs roamed more than 60 million years ago, as evidenced by the

> ## The second largest oil reserves in the world

rich fossil finds along the Red Deer River. Today large herds of cattle graze there – in peaceful harmony with the oil pumps that extract Alberta's black gold. With the huge deposits of tar sands around Fort McMurray in northern Alberta, Canada has the second largest oil reserves in the world, after Saudi Arabia. There and on the large wheat fields in the southern part of the region it is clear that the economy largely depends on agriculture and the abundant raw materials. Demand for raw materials has created a boom in the western provinces of Canada in recent years, even during the global crisis of 2009 – but this is also because the banks in Canada are comparatively conservative and prudent.

In the far north there are the sparsely green mountain ranges and valleys of the Yukon and the Northwest Territories. About 100 years ago this was where the greatest gold rush in history took place – and since forgotten. The climatic contrasts here are as varied as the landscapes: damp, mild marine climate prevails on the Pacific coast, in the interior of Canada however, there is a continental climate with hot summers and bitterly cold winters. High in the Arctic North, summer barely lasts two months while in the south – on the same latitude as the French wine region of Champagne – the Okanagan Valley in British Columbia is temperate enough for vineyards and peach orchards to thrive. But even the extreme heat of summer, in the prairies of Alberta, and the polar cold of the Arctic winter, are tempered by the low humidity.

1778
The British Explorer James Cook explores the Pacific coast

1792/93
Alexander Mackenzie crosses the continent to the Pacific Ocean

1821
North West Company of Montreal and Hudson's Bay Company merge, their combined territory make the company was the largest private landowner in the world

1867
The birth of Canada: in the British North America Act the colonies of Ontario, Québec, Nova Scotia and New Brunswick are declared the Dominion of Canada

Only about 34 million people live in Canada, only around 8 million in the entire western region. There is a lot of space left and the vast area is ideal for camping, fishing, hiking, canoeing and horse riding. But it need not only be all about the wilderness experience. You also need to see the towns and cities. Vancouver – surrounded by the sea – is considered one of the most beautiful cities on the North American continent. The few cities are also the only enclaves of modern civilization in western Canada. Only the south, the region along the border with the United States, is made accessible by highways and settlements. About 80 per cent of the population lives in the fertile valley of the Fraser River, in the temperate valleys around Kelowna and Kamloops and in Alberta's prairies. However, the northern and Arctic areas are almost deserted.

**Hot summers and bitterly cold winters**

The western region of Canada is the youngest part of the country – both historically and geographically. Only 30 million years ago the Rocky Mountains were thrust upward from the sedimentary layers of the ancient seas. The continental drift of the Pacific Plate against the North American mainland forced up a series of mountain ranges, this area is known as the Pacific Cordillera and is the youngest of Canada's geographic regions. Roughly 30,000 years ago the ancestors of the Native Americans moved across the Bering Strait and then through western Canada and from there settled throughout the rest of the continent. Their descendants are still strongly represented in the region today. They live in small villages in their old tribal areas, and are managing their rights and indentity with growing self-confidence; this is especially evident along the western coast where their totem poles and plank houses can still still be admired.

Much later, some 200 years ago, the first white explorers, the British Captain Cook and Captain Vancouver, sailed along the west coast and began the fur trade with the Native Americans. At the beginning of the 19th century the first real settlers arrived: farmers from the Ukraine, from England, Germany and Scandinavia. And just 120 years ago the first cities arose, and the first railway from Montréal steamed westwards.

Economically the Canadians in the west have remained true to the land: mining, ranching, fisheries, wheat and more recently the cultivation of ginseng are the main industries in the south of the provinces. In the relatively unexplored north forestry is

**1871**
British Columbia joins the Dominion of Canada

**1885**
Completion of the Trans-Canada railway line. Banff, the first Canadian National Park, is established

**1898**
Gold rush at Klondike. First oil find in Alberta

**1931**
Canada is a sovereign state in the Commonwealth

**1942**
Construction of the Alaska Highway

**1962**
Completion of the Trans-Canada Highway

The distinctive black and white orcas are often seen around Vancouver Island

the mainstay, which currently provides plenty of work with the cutting down of dead trees infected by the bark beetle. Still, there are huge, totally unspoilt and uninhabited landscapes, in part under permanent conservation, such as the nearly 4000 square miles of Tweedsmuir Provincial Park.

Western Canada is a paradise for wildlife enthusiasts. There are endless opportunities for adventure. But not all of them require you to tests the limits of your own resilience – a comfortable tour in a camper can also give you a sense of

**A paradise for wildlife enthusiasts**

freedom and space. Because a holiday in Canada it is not all about ticking off attractions and sights but rather about taking your time and enjoying long hikes in the mountains, exploring wild beaches, relaxing with a campfire barbecue or just breathing in the clean air of this unspoilt country.

| 1965 | 1988 | 1990s | 2007 | 2012 |
|------|------|-------|------|------|
| Canada adopts the maple leaf national flag | Olympic Winter Games in Calgary | A wave of immigration from Hong Kong brings 70,000 Chinese to Vancouver | The economy booms due to skyrocketing oil and commodity prices | In the north of British Columbia the Endbridge Pipeline project triggers protests from conservationists |

# WHAT'S HOT

## 1 Eye-catching

*Art* Not only the works of art are worth seeing, but also the exhibition rooms, such as the *Van Dop Gallery (421 Richmond St., New Westminster, photo)*, integrated into the rooms of a private house – living with art is the motto. About 50 studios, galleries and cafés form part of *Art Central (100 7th Ave. SW, Calgary)*. The *Vancouver Art Gallery (750 Hornby St.)* regularly transforms itself into a hot party location with very whacky performances. The *Hotel Arts (119 12th Ave. SW, Calgary)* is the perfect choice for music lovers.

## 2 Downhill

*Sport* A kitewing *(www.kitewing.com)* attatched to skis, snowboard or skates lets you fly over the snowfields. While a Dirtsurfer, an inline board, means you don't even need the snow to have some fun. At *Sooke Cycle (2075 Anna Marie Rd., Sooke)* you can rent or buy the boards. The Splitboard is brand new *(www.splitboard.com)*, a snowboard separated vertically into two parts. The board allows you to also go uphill and – once clipped together – to whiz back down. The Kootneays are a popular area for it.

## 3 Tasty

*Culinary* Vancouver's Gastown is a culinary meeting place, a tasting tour *(www.vancouverfoodtour.com, photo)* will give you an overview of what is on offer, then seafood fans can head over to the *Cork and Fin (221 Carrall St.)* or to enjoy Spanish tapas in *Judas Goat Taberna (27 Blood Alley)*. There are more tasty snacks in the *Acme Café (51 Hastings St. W)*. Even if your belt now needs loosening, do not miss out on the pies!

## Calgary rocks

*Music* Canada's third largest city takes first place over Toronto and Vancouver in all matters music. It is the home to a thriving music scene and the hometown of *The Dudes (www.thedudesmusic.ca)*. Live music here is not impersonal halls but rather in pubs with stages, such as in the popular *Ship & Anchor (534 17th Ave) SW)*, the *Drum and Monkey (1201 1st St. SW)* and *Broken City (613 11th Ave) SW)*. The concert venues become crowded in June when the *Sled Island Music and Arts Festival (www.sledisland.com)* attracts all sorts of outlandish and flamboyant musicians to the city.

## Two in one

*Shopping* Multi-purpose stores are part of the Canadian way. A visit to Vancouver *Mr. Lee's General Store (109 E. Broadway)* is a step back to the 1930s. In the trendy store you can buy retro leather products, sweets and stationery items. There is also fresh coffee, and downstairs you can visit a barber. Not only can you get a shave in the *BeautyBar (2142 W 4th Ave.)*, but also buy jewellery or have a make-up demonstration. In Calgary the *Tubby Dog (1022 17th Ave. SW)* eatery also hosts concerts, has art on the walls and arcade games from the 1980s. In Edmonton you can buy environmentally friendly baby clothes and support ethical manufacture when you shop in the *Carbon Environmental Boutique (10184 104 St.)* while the *AntiSocial (2337 Main St.)* in Vancouver sells skateboard gear, clothing as well as street art.

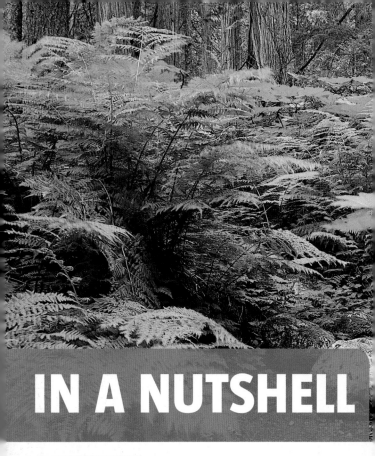

# IN A NUTSHELL

## ARCHITECTURE

Vancouver has changed architecturally in recent years and it now has a forest of new glass and steel high-rise buildings and Olympic structures such as the ecologically designed media centre, which is now a conference venue. Other iconic buildings in Vancouver are the public library, designed by Moshe Safie (1995) and the cruise ship terminal Canada Place created by Ed Zeidler in 1986 with its distinctive white roof sails. And there is also False Creek, a uniquely curved construction by Arthur Erickson that rises up next to the otherwise rather unimaginative glass apartment towers. The late architect (he passed away in 2009) also built the UBC Museum of Anthropology and Waterfall House at the entrance to Granville Island.

And the most famous building in Calgary is without doubt the Saddledome rodeo arena with its sweeping roof.

## ENVIRONMENTAL PROTECTION

Sustainability is the key word of the Canadian organic movement. Despite the fact that the conservative government in Ottawa opted out of the Kyoto Protocol for climate protection – many Canadians see themselves as being environmen-

Photo: Revelstoke National Park

Once the realm of the bison, today the breadbasket of Canada – here is some background information on the region

tally conscious. Rubbish is separated and recycled, nature parks are created and environmental organizations are actively supported. While western Canada is the birthplace of powerful environmental organizations – such as the *David Suzuki Foundation*, *Living Oceans Society* and *Greenpeace* – the country is still one of the world's largest squanderers. No wonder, because the Canadians have always had

an abundant supply of mineral resources, energy, and water but they are now re-thinking their ways. Learn more about environmental issues in Canada: *thegreen pages.ca*.

# FLORA & FAUNA

Most of western Canada lies in the area of the boreal forest, which stretches in a broad band across the continent. These forests are the habitat of bears, moose, several deer, lynxes, porcupines and beavers, and more recently the bark beetle – possibly a result of global warming – which is wreaking havoc in the interior of British Columbia. To the north, the forests of taiga and tundra extend into the Yukon and the Northwest Territories. Only caribou, mountain hares and musk ox can live off the sparse lichens and mosses in this region. However, in the summer the large freshwater areas nourish countless waterfowl.

The south and east of Alberta form part of the large North American prairie, originally a grass savannah, but due to its fertile soil the area is now mostly ploughed and covered in massive crop fields. What was once the home to millions of bison is today the breadbasket of Canada – there are bison in only a few protected areas. Alpine flora, with many wild flowers, flourishes in the Rocky Mountains providing nourishment to mountain goats and sheep. On the western slopes of the Coast Mountains and on Vancouver Island there are lush rainforests full of tall Douglas firs, Sitka spruces, red cedars and lush ferns.

# GOLD

After the publication of Jack of London's novels almost everyone knows the story of the Klondike gold rush. Actually the search for the precious metal played a very special role in Canadian history, because the discovery of gold opened up the whole western region. Around 1860 the gold rush in the Cariboo Mountains attracted thousands of miners. 30 years later the call of 'Gold in the Yukon!' and 100,000 gold diggers toiled laboriously through ice and snow in the Coast Mountains, to reach the promised land in time for spring. In just three years gold worth 100 million dollars was found and Dawson City became the largest city west of Winnipeg with 30,000 inhabitants.

Gold is still being mined to this day – in Klondike, in Yellowknife and in the hard granite rock of the Canadian Shield in eastern Canada – some four million ounces annually, of which a large part goes to the *Maple Leaf Dollar*, one of the best selling gold coins in the world.

# ICE HOCKEY

The seamen who travelled with the English explorer John Franklin during the 19th century supposedly played hockey on the ice thus establishing today's most popular sport in Canada. When the home teams play off for the famous Stanley Cup, then the whole country is in hockey fever. Currently the most popular teams are the *Vancouver Canucks* and the *Montréal Canadians*.

# MUSIC

When Peter Fonda made the famous road trip movie 'Easy Rider' the bikers cruised along on the open road to the legendary 'Born to be Wild' song. The soundtrack was by the band Steppenwolf and the members mostly came from Toronto. A typical case in point as Canada has never created their own independent pop music, Hollywood and America were too dominant which is why many Canadian artists such as Leonard Cohen, Neil Young and Joni Mitchell all moved down to the States. The Canadian musicians that are currently famous include Bryan Adams, Céline Dion, Sarah McLachlan, Alanis Morissette, Avril Lavigne, Nelly Furtado and country singer Shania Twain.

# NATIONAL PARKS

The forerunner of present-day Banff National Park was founded in 1885 'for the benefit, advantage and enjoyment of the people of Canada'. It was the first in what is now a long list of parks, where the most beautiful and most pristine regions of the vast countryside are protected. The ecological aspects of the park system, mandated by the Canadian ministry of the environment, were considered ence; you will be liable for a fine of up to C$500. Hunting is naturally also prohibited. However, you may fish in the streams and lakes – with a fishing license of course. For additional information see: *www.parks canada.ca*

Traditional meeting of chiefs: powwow festival of the Blackfoot Indians

to be groundbreaking. The country's 42 national parks today cover a total of more than 88,000 square miles and a further dozen parks are planned, as every ecologically important region of Canada will be placed under the protection of a nature reserve.

Approximately 30 million people visit the parks annually and those that do must abide by park rules: no animals may fed, no branch broken. Picking a bouquet of wild flowers can be an expensive experi-

## NATIVE AMERICAN & INUIT

The ancestors of the Native Americans probably came across the Bering Strait to North America 35,000–15,000 years ago. Over the course of millennia they spread across the continent and developed into independent cultural groups, with the semi-nomadic hunter tribes living in the north. The Plains Indians (in present day Alberta) followed the massive herds of buffalo, while the Kwakiutl and Haida on the west coast had such a rich food supply that they had enough leisure time to become skilled woodcarvers. The ancestors of today's Inuit crossed the Canadian Arctic from Alaska about 1000 years ago. When the Europeans started arriving in the 15th century they introduced diseases that decimated the local inhabitants and then, with the settlement of the west in the 19th century, the Native Americans were pushed out into reserves. Half-hearted efforts were made to make the reserves economically independent as the goal of the Europeans was the integration of the Native Americans, not support for their independence and maintenance of their cultural heritage. Now known as the 'First Nations' in Canada, there are around 700,000 Native Americans and 50,000 Inuit in the country. Their rights as the original inhabitants of the continent were acknowledged with a section in the 1982 Constitution Act. This, and the strengthening self-confidence of indigenous people, led to numerous movements for land restitution and self-governance. The Inuit achieved the most spectacular success with this – in 1999 they received their own territory separate from the Northwest Territories, known as *Nunavut* (our land). Nunavut is almost exclusively governed and managed by Inuit.

# ORGANIC FOOD

Fit and healthy living is part of the Canadian west coast lifestyle and organic food and products are not only found in health food stores but also in supermarket chains such as Vancouver's Whole Foods, Urban Fair or Calgary's Planet Organic, as well as in the numerous small markets. Menus in restaurants will often have 'grass fed' or 'free range' listed next to meat, eggs, and dairy products.

# POLITICS

Canada is a federal constitutional monarchy and part of the British Commonwealth with Queen Elizabeth II as the country's Head of State with ceremonial duties. The country's ten provinces have extensive autonomy, in matters of education, cultural policy, health care, and use of natural resources. Only the three sparsely populated territories in the north are financed and governed largely from the federal capital of Ottawa.

# RCMP (MOUNTIES)

Dressed in red, the *Royal Canadian Mounted Police* are probably Canada's most famous and recognised symbol. In their parade uniform the Mounties perform at official events and appear in many souvenir photographs. However, they are

# INNOVATIVE CANADIANS

Telephone, matches, and the zip – did you know that they all come from Canada? And the Canadians have invented a whole lot more, such as the snowmobile and the combine harvester. In 1879 the enormous size of western Canada led the railway engineer Sanford Fleming to divide the earth into 24 time zones. Canada has also contributed with medical innovations: in 1929 Frederick Banting and Charles Best developed the diabetes drug insulin and the engineer John Hopps developed the first pacemaker in 1951. Today Canadian researchers are at the forefront of AIDS and genetic research.

much more than just a colourful accessory, today the highly trained federal police are responsible for all rural regions and jurisdictions in Canada that cannot afford their own police – and there are many are in the sparsely populated west. Founded and totem poles now stand in front of government buildings and museums. Kitsch plastic replicas decorate the souvenir shops. Totem poles the most recognisable symbol of Native American culture. Originally, this highly developed wood

In some areas of Canada the Mounties still patrol on horseback

in 1873, the RCMP force is today about 15,000 strong. For decades, the forts of the Mounties were also the only outposts of civilization in the then rather wild west. The lawmen patrolled the Arctic with dog sleds, on horseback and by canoe, and went into the most isolated gold mining camps. And even today you can experience the Mounties up close and personal – as armed guards on the highways that will fine you and read you the riot act if you exceed the speed limit!

## TOTEM POLES

Native American carving and sculpture has grown popular in recent years, the elaborate masks, mythical animals carving art was only in the culture of the Northwest Coast Indians, roughly in the area between Vancouver Island and southeast Alaska. The totem poles were not religious icons but rather symbols of prestige, the vehicle for a clan or a chief to demonstrate power and wealth. For decades the 'pagan carvings' were banned by the state and missionaries but this ancient art form is now undergoing a revival. You can see the most beautiful totem poles in the museums of Vancouver and Victoria. Or you can take a drive to the Native American villages up the west coast, where many original totem poles have been preserved, such as in Alert Bay, Quadra Island and Hazelton.

# FOOD & DRINK

**There is no Canadian national dish, the immigrant groups who came from all continents were too different, the country too large. Instead it is the diversity of specialities that is the charm of the multicultural culinary delights of western Canada.**

In all the major cities, you will be able to enjoy excellent Chinese, Indian and Italian restaurants. There is also sushi; the fresh fish from the Pacific is of the highest quality, making sushi a very popular choice. Aside from fresh salmon (in many varieties) there is, of course, also Canada's famous grilled steak often served with baked potatoes and corn on the cob.

Of course you will also be confronted with the usual fast foods, the monotony of hamburgers and grilled chicken. There are fast food restaurants serving breakfast and lunch everywhere in Canada. But if you put a little effort in and look beyond the flashing neon signs you will find smaller venues offering home cooked meals – in the small fish restaurants on Vancouver Island, in rustic lodges in the wilderness or in ethnic restaurants in the cities – and then you will be pleasantly surprised.

In Alberta, you have to try a steak – either in restaurant or barbecued on your own campfire. The cattle range wild on huge ranches and the meat is unsurpassable,

Canada's culinary charms lie in the diversity of local ingredients and the recipes brought here by the immigrants

and the portions are designed for hungry lumberjacks. West of the Rocky Mountains seafood is the main culinary attraction, deliciously fresh on Vancouver Island and along the Sunshine Coast north of Vancouver. Poached or grilled salmon (the best is Coho) with fresh vegetables from the Fraser Valley and a crisp white wine from the sunny Okanagan Valley is among the finest that Canada has to offer.

In the style of the new Californian cuisine that emerged in the 1970s in San Francisco and Los Angeles, Vancouver and Victoria have developed a similar West Coast style. The methods of preparation and the spices used come from all over the world – from France as well as from Asia. The produce is however, ecologically sound i.e. locally grown. Salad leaves and vegetables from the Fraser Valley, peaches, apples and

# LOCAL SPECIALITIES

▶ **Bannock** – Scottish flat bread baked in a pan (adapted by the Native Americans as fry bread)
▶ **Beavertail** – fried pastry sprinkled with cinnamon and sugar
▶ **Buffalo wings** – despite the name this is actually chicken wings, marinated in a spicy sauce, and then either fried or grilled as a snack (photo left)
▶ **Butter tart** – a pioneer pastry tart with a butter, syrup and sugar filling. These small, individual tarts are considered to be one of the few genuinely Canadian recipes
▶ **Caesar** – a drink made of vodka and clam juice served with celery and lime in a celery salt rimmed glass
▶ **Cedar planked salmon** – salmon that is grilled on a water soaked plank of cedar

▶ **Clam/seafood chowder** – hearty cream-based mussel/fish soup
▶ **Dungeness crab** – large species of crab prized for its very sweet meat
▶ **Hash browns** – finely grated potatoes that are pan fried
▶ **Nanaimo bar** – a rich dessert bar that originated in Nanaimo, BC
▶ **Pacific salmon** – there are numerous different species such as Sockeye, Pink, Chum, Coho and Chinook – a popular dish in many restaurants
▶ **Poutine** – potato chips topped with curd cheese cubes and doused with gravy
▶ **Saskatoon berries** – native to the Canadian prairies and British Columbia, they are similar to blueberries

grapes from the Okanagan Valley, crab, halibut and salmon from the Pacific, right on their doorstep.

The talented young chefs understand how best to make the different flavours harmonize and how best to bring out the different tastes. And sometimes, they also include traditional cooking methods such as when the salmon is grilled in the Native American way – on planks of cedar – and

dessert is ice cream with wild berries. Your best bet for breakfast is in a coffee shop. Some of them are part of the hotel or are situated close to the motels. You can either enjoy a small continental breakfast or order a large American breakfast with eggs and fried potatoes, or pancakes which are usually served with maple syrup. Coffee is filled up free of charge, but often it is a watery brew. For lunch, roughly between noon and 2pm, the Canadians often eat smaller dishes, which are listed on a separate lunch menu, often a simple salad or soup and sandwich.

In the rural regions, dinner is often served early between 5.30pm and 7pm, in the larger cities between 7pm and 10pm. In most restaurants you will need to wait to be shown you to your table.

After dinner the final amount of the bill may not be what you anticipated: the prices shown on the menu do not include the tax, which differs from province to province and it is only shown on the bill. The tip is also usually not included and if you are happy with the service then a 15–20 per cent tip is the norm.

In addition to the global American fast food chains, there are also some local ones: *Earls* and the *Cactus Club* – popular restaurant chain in the greater Vancouver area – offer excellent dishes that range from pasta to steaks and omelettes. With its dark wood interiors, *The Keg* chain is famous for good (but not exactly cheap) steaks. And if you feel like a hamburger, then one of the branches of *Triple O White Spot* is a good choice. They serve good quality food at reasonable prices; they also freshly bake their donuts baked and have decadent milkshakes. For a quick shot of energy lots of Canadians pop into a *Tim Hortons*. The coffee and doughnut chain is more popular than Starbucks and in addition to good coffee and freshly baked doughnuts; they also have a selection of affordable soups and sandwiches. If there is a national drink in Canada, then it is beer – aromatic and very palatable especially when compared to the rather watery American beer – which goes well with a hearty steak. Everywhere in the country you will find *Molson Canadian* or *Labatt's Blue* while specialty beers such as *Kokanee* are served only in some regions. In recent years micro breweries have also

become increasingly popular. In British Columbia you should try the beers by *Okanagan Spring* and *Granville Island Camp.* In Alberta, try beers by the *Wild Rose Brewing Company,* many of the smaller places such as Canmore and Jasper have their own small breweries.

Canada's national drink: beer

Wine is served in most restaurants; good wines from California or France are often listed. However, it is definitely worthwhile trying the local wine from the Okanagan Valley or from the Niagara Peninsula. If you like stronger drinks, you can rely on the excellent Canadian whiskey, which is either served on the rocks or – just like rum or gin – in mixed drinks. A specialty of the north is *Yukon Jack,* a devastatingly strong whiskey liqueur ideal for the long, cold winter nights.

In addition to the usual hotel bars there are also many rustic bars with a pool table and a long bar counter: often the best place to meet the locals. A Canadian feature is the cabaret, not the usual kind of cabaret, instead the venue is a large bar and the performance is a country and western band.

# SHOPPING

Western Canada is not necessarily a well known shopping destination, but once you arrive you will be enticed by the wide selection of goods available. In the cities there is an excellent variety of shops, in the hinterland though your options decrease dramatically. A small grocery store that also sells shoes and chainsaws, or a gas station with a few shelves of items has to suffice in the small little towns. It is best to stock your camper with groceries and equipment before you go on a long trip. The further north you go the more expensive everything becomes.

## CHEAP & TRENDY

Casual wear, sports shoes and sporting goods are cheaper than in Europe – even if the exchange rate is not in your favour. The outlet shopping that is so popular in North America is still widely unknown in western Canada, with the exception of a few malls between Calgary and Edmonton. The Canadian chain *Winners* has branches in many of the cities and specialises in discount sales of old stock and they have cheap jeans and children's clothing.

Canadian sportswear brands such as *Lululemon Athletica* and *Roots Canada* are very popular with the fashion-conscious youth, but they are more expensive.

## CULINARY

Regional products such as jam or wine from the Okanagan Valley, wild flower honey from the prairies or smoked salmon are popular souvenirs. There is also salmon in unusual ways such as tinned smoked mousse or the delicious Indian Candy, salmon that has been candied and smoked. The most famous Canadian souvenir is maple syrup. The thickened sap from maple trees usually comes from the deciduous forests in the eastern regions and is an essential part of a hearty pancake breakfast in Canada.

## MALLS & OLD TOWN DISTRICT

Shopping malls, departments stores and boutiques are everywhere in the major cities. Renovated old harbour waterfront districts are ideal for strolling and shopping such as Granville Island in Vancouver or

## Native American and Inuit carvings and sculptures are popular – and expensive – but there are other options too

the old town district Victoria with restaurants, art galleries and cafés.

### NATIVE AMERICAN ART

Native American and Inuit arts and crafts are popular but not cheap, the best option is to buy directly in the reserves, in reputable galleries or in the shops of the major museums. The west coast tribes, once famous for their totem poles, today carve smaller objects such as masks or bowls and also use the traditional stylized animal symbols found in their art in silver jewellery and drawings. Native Americans in the northern regions traditionally make moccasins from moose leather, woven baskets decorated with porcupine quills as well as beaded leather jackets. The Inuit of the Arctic are famous for their beautiful sculptures made from soapstone, whalebone and caribou antlers, which are sold in the galleries of the large cities (at prices from about C$300).

### REGIONAL GIFTS

In the coastal villages of Vancouver Island and in Vancouver, you will find the beautiful, chunky Cowichan sweaters and all kinds of handicrafts items made of wood, clay and ceramic. Many artists, who usually exhibit their works in the galleries of Victoria, live mainly on the Gulf Islands off Vancouver Island. Ideal souvenirs from Alberta are cowboy items: top quality Stetson hats, silver belt buckles and handmade boots. Many shops offer a good selection to choose from and you can even have a pair of boots custom-made. All over Alberta and British Columbia you will also find traditional checked lumberjack shirts that are good during the trip for protection against mosquitoe bites.

# THE PERFECT ROUTE

## CALGARY AND THE PRAIRIE

Take a day to the get settled in ① *Calgary* → p. 81. Stroll around Stephen Avenue Mall and do some affordable shopping, because there is no provincial tax in Alberta. Then head for Hwy. 9 and the wide, flat prairies and make a detour to ② *Drumheller* → p. 84 and the spectacular dinosaur finds in the Red Deer River valley. On the way back via Hwy. 56/Hwy. 1 make another a stop for the interactive exhibits in the Blackfoot Crossing Park — and for a bison burger.

## IN THE ROCKIES

From Calgary the Trans-Canada Highway heads for the Rocky Mountains, the snow-covered 3000m/9850ft peaks of ③ *Banff National Park* → p. 67, glacial lakes such as Lake Louise and a magnificent scenic road, the *Icefields Parkway* → p. 69, 99. You should stay on this road as far as the Athabasca glacier in the ④ *Jasper National Park* → p. 73. Thereafter you can head back down southwards and continue on Hwy. 1 across the spine of the Rockies to the ⑤ *Yoho National Park* → p. 78 and the spectacular Takakkaw Falls, its 344m/1130ft drop making it the second highest in Canada.

## OKANAGAN VALLEY WINE

The smaller national parks of ⑥ *Glacier* → p. 54 and *Revelstoke* → p. 57 (photo left) accompany Hwy. 1 westwards with views of picturesque mountains and forests. Branch off to the south to the wine region of ⑦ *Okanagan Valley* → p. 58, where numerous wineries around Kelowna and Penticton make some very good wines. Take a break to indulge in a little wine tasting in the wineries (tip: the Mission Hill Winery in Westbank), delicious lunches in terrace restaurants and bathing in the warm lakes.

## OLYMPIC MEMORIES

Now to the BC ranch country where it is desert dry and almost always sunny. On Hwy. 5A, 8, and 1 the route meanders north past lonely hills to the Fraser River Canyon. To cool off why not go white water rafting at ⑧ *Lytton* → p. 56 (photo right). From the river Hwy. 99 then climbs up to the sparsely populated Coast Mountains to ⑨ *Whistler* → p. 62, the venue of the 2010 Winter Olympics, where you can take time for a trip up Whistler Mountain, a bike tour or a round of golf.

Experience the many facets of western Can[...]
on a trip from Calgary to Vancouver and the
Pacific with detours off the main route

## IN THE RAINFOREST

At the north end of the Howe Sound the Squamish Estuary comes into sight and shortly thereafter is Horseshoe Bay and the large car ferry to ⑩ *Nanaimo* → p. 43 to the onward journey to Vancouver Island. Directly north of the city, are some attractive bathing beaches, but an even more beautiful detour is via Hwy. 4 to the wild west coast and the ⑪ *Pacific Rim National Park* → p. 44. You can easily spend a few days in the park's three separate regions: kayaking, whale and bear watching and hiking in the rainforest.

## THE SCENIC AND TEMPERATE SOUTH

Back in Nanaimo Hwy. 17 now follows the coast southwards via ⑫ *Duncan* → p. 42, a large cultural centre of the Cowichan Indians, on to ⑬ *Victoria* → p. 47, the lovely seaside provincial capital of BC. Take a stroll around Inner Harbour, a boat ride to see orca, or a car or bike ride through the lush seaside residential area.

## AT YOUR DESTINATION: VANCOUVER

Yet another ferry ride, this time from Swartz Bay back to the mainland, and ⑭ *Vancouver* → p. 32. You should set aside at least one or two days you to explore this beautiful metropolis: sightseeing in Gastown, Granville Island and Robson Street, to a bike ride in Stanley Park – and of course for a gourmet dinner with fresh wild salmon.

About 2600km/1615mi
Pure driving time: 41 hours
Recommended duration: two weeks.
Detailed map of the route on the back cover, in the road atlas and the pull-out map

# VANCOUVER

### ⬡ MAP INSIDE BACK COVER
A no more beautiful place to set off on a round trip through the west than Vancouver (133 D5) *(ℳ E14)*, the city of the 2010 Winter Olympics.

What San Francisco is for west coast of the United States, so Vancouver is for Canada: a young, vibrant city with a captivating charm and casual, European flair, a dynamic metropolis set against a dramatic backdrop of dark green mountains in the broad river delta of the Fraser River, with restored Victorian homes, spacious parks, beaches and plenty of unspoilt nature in the surrounding countryside. With approximately 2.3 million inhabitants (the

### 🏙 WHERE TO START?
The best place to start is **Robson Square**, the central square of the city. Here the Robson Street shopping district starts toward the west and north is the old town around Water Street, Canada Place and the waterfront Seawalk. Also within walking distance are Yaletown, and the beaches in the vibrant West End neighbouring Denman Street and Stanley Park. Parking garage in the Pacific Centre Mall, corner of Robson and Granville streets.

Photo: Granville Island and Burrard Bridge

**Jewel of the Pacific: between the ocean and a breathtaking mountain backdrop lies the cultural metropolis of western Canada**

greater metropolitan area of the Fraser Delta) Vancouver is today the largest city in western Canada. The city's more than 150km/93mi of port facilities makes it the most important economic and commercial centre on the Pacific coast. Three renowned universities, numerous museums, theatres and galleries also make it the cultural hub of the region. In recent years so many films and TV shows have been shot in the city that it now has the nickname of 'Hollywood North'.

This dynamic city is still surprisingly young. When Captain George Vancouver discovered the mouth of the Fraser River on the Pacific coast in 1792 – and soon sailed on – there were only huge Douglas fir forests. Years later, in 1860, a small logging camp was established on the shores of Burrard Inlet. Then in 1886, when it became the terminus of the transcontinental railway, Vancouver took off.

During the world trade fair Expo 86 the city showcased what she had become: a set routes. You can hop on and off whenever you want to and they come along every 30 minutes *(daily 9am–6pm | ticket C$38)*.

Traditionally landscaped: Dr. Sun Yat-Sen Classical Chinese Garden

very liveable, natural metropolis, an oasis of fine urban culture in the midst of the wilderness of western Canada.

You should set aside at least two days to explore Vancouver: a day for an extended stroll through the city centre area and a day for a trip to the museums and attractions in the city's outskirts.

## SIGHTSEEING

A good initial overview of the city is to be had from the *The Lookout* tower on top of the ✹ *Harbour Centre* (U E3) *(∭ e3)* on Hastings Street or – even better – gondola ride on the aerial tramway system up ✹ *Grouse Mountain* with spectacular views of the city. Back on the ground you should hop on the Vancouver trolleys that go to all the city centre attractions on two

### CANADA PLACE ⭐ (U E3) *(∭ e3)*

During the Expo 86 the pier, with its snow-white tent design by architect Ed Zeidler, was the Canada Pavilion. Today it is ideal for a stroll, to watch the cruise ships coming and going and to enjoy the view over the fjord from the top of the ✹ pier *(Cordova St./Howe St.)*. Vancouver aims to be the 'greenest' city in Canada and this is demonstrated with the sustainable technology and design used for the 2010 international of media centre of the 🕓 *Vancouver Convention Centre,* where the *Olympic Torch* on the western side is a reminder of the winter games.

### CAPILANO SALMON HATCHERY ●
### (133 D5) *(∭ E14)*

Here you can view the life cycle of salmon through underwater gallery windows and information panels. From mid August, the adult salmon return. *Daily in the summer 8am–8pm | admission free | North Vancouver | Capilano Rd.*

## CAPILANO SUSPENSION BRIDGE ☼
(133 D5) (*ⅆ E14*)

A swaying, almost 140m/460ft long suspension bridge spans the 70m/230ft deep canyon. There is also a totem pole park, a nature trail in the treetops and a spectacular cliff walk high above the gorge. However, this tourist attraction draws crowds of visitors. *Daily in summer 9am–8pm,, otherwise 9am–5pm | admission C$30 | North Vancouver | Capilano Rd.*

## CHINATOWN (U F4) (*ⅆ f4*)

The neighbourhood around Pender and Main Street is home to the largest Chinese community (aside from San Francisco's Chinatown) in North America. Worth a visit is the *Dr. Sun Yat-Sen Classical Chinese Garden* on Carr Street. On Friday to Sunday evenings there is the *Chinatown Night Market* on Keefer Street (between Main and Columbia) with stalls, vendors, food and entertainment. Also well worth a visit is the modern INSIDER TIP ▶ *T & T Supermarket (corner Keefer/Abbott St.)* which offers every imaginable Asian product. The next door area of Hastings Street has lots of vagrants – it is not dangerous, but also not very nice.

## GASTOWN (U E4) (*ⅆ e4*)

This district is the restored old town of Vancouver with a boundary along Water Street. The old brick buildings now house shops, restaurants and art galleries. A fun attraction is the *Steam Clock* on the corner of Cambie Street, which is powered by steam from the municipal heating network. A statue of city founder John 'Gassy Jack' Deighton is just east, at the Water/Carr Street intersection. He is thought to have built the first house in Vancouver in 1867 – a saloon. This established a tradition and today there are still numerous pubs around the square.

## GRANVILLE ISLAND
(U B–C6) (*ⅆ b–c6*)

The restored waterfront harbour area under the Granville Bridge is another attractive area in Vancouver: do some shopping at the famous ● *Public Market*, browse colourful art shops like the *Gallery of BC Ceramics (1359 Cartwright St.)* or eat ice cream with a view of houseboats and city skyline. Not to be missed: INSIDER TIP ▶ Railspur Alley with artist studios, innovative galleries and a small café.

## MARITIME MUSEUM (U A5) (*ⅆ a5*)

The crown in the museum's jewel is the 'St. Roch', an Arctic patrol ship. The wooden

### ★ Canada Place
Built for Expo 86 and now a hub of activity with harbour promenade, cafés and great views → p. 34

### ★ Stanley Park
The most beautiful urban park in Canada – ideal for a bike ride → p. 36

### ★ UBC Museum of Anthropology
Original totem poles and masks of the Northwest Coast Native Americans → p. 36

### ★ Bridges
Popular meeting place in the late afternoon – views over the water and chic clientele → p. 37

MARCO POLO HIGHLIGHTS

schooner traversed the Northwest Passage several times. *June–Sept daily 10am–5pm, otherwise Tue–Sat, Sun only from noon | admission C$11 | 1100 Chestnut St.*

Tribal history immortalised: totem poles in Stanley Park

## QUEEN ELIZABETH PARK 🔆
(133 D5) *(₥ E14)*

Beautiful garden in an old stone quarry and the best panoramic view of Vancouver. The domed building at the top of the hill has a botanical garden, the *Bloedel Conservatory. Admission C$5 | Cambie St./ 33rd Ave.*

## STANLEY PARK ★ (U A–D1) *(₥ a–d1)*

A beautiful urban park with hiking trails and picnic areas where there are some original totem poles surrounded by a dense forest of ancient Douglas firs. Built in 1938 the *Lions Gate Bridge,* at the northern tip of the park, connects the city to North Vancouver. The 1000 acre park also incorporates the ● *Vancouver Aquarium* with beluga whales, sea otters, and an exhibition on the migration of salmon *(summer daily 9.30am–7pm, otherwise until 5pm | admission C$27, in winter C$21)*. You can cycle around the peninsula, on which the park is situated, on the 10km/6mi long 🔆 ● *Stanley Park Drive (bicycle rental near the Denman St. entrance | C$21–65 for half a day)*. End of June to early September the Native American *Klahowya Village (admission C$8)* has artisans and dance performances *(Fri–Sun)*.

## UBC MUSEUM OF ANTHROPOLOGY ★
(133 D5) *(₥ E14)*

The unconventional museum building by Arthur Erickson, in the grounds of the University of British Columbia, houses an important collection of totem poles and masks of the Northwest Coast Native Americans. Beautiful historic carvings from Argyllit as well as modern works by Bill Reid. *Daily in summer 10am–5pm, Tue 10am–9pm, Oct–mid May closed Mon | admission C$16.75 | 6393 NW Marine Dr.*

## VANCOUVER MUSEUM (U A5) *(₥ a5)*

The large Rotunda on the shore of English Bay exhibits the history of the city of Vancouver, the natural history of the area as well as Native American craftwork. Adjacent is the *MacMillan Space Centre & Planetarium,* with evening laser shows. *Daily 10am–5pm, Thu 10am–8pm, winter closed Mon | admission C$12 | 1100 Chestnut St.*

## VAN DUSEN BOTANICAL GARDEN
(133 D5) *(₥ E14)*

Covering 55 acres and is full of plants, flowers, groves, idyllic paths and small lakes. The garden is particularly colourful from May to July. *Daily 9am–sunset, in winter from 10am | admission C$10.75 | 5251 Oak St.*

**INSIDER TIP YALETOWN** (U D5) (𝒟 d5)

The city's trendy district: during the day the quirky boutiques along Hamilton and Mainland Street attract visitors and then at night it is the chic restaurants, brew pubs and bars.

## FOOD & DRINK

**BRIDGES** ★ ⭝⭝ (U B6) (𝒟 b6)

Lovely bistro with a large terrace on the water and wonderful views of the city. *1696 Duranleau St. | Granville Island | tel. 604 6 87 44 00 | www.bridgesrestaurant. com | Budget–Expensive*

**CAFFE ARTIGIANO** (U D3) (𝒟 d3)

Popular café chain with excellent cappuccino, breakfast and snacks; there is a branches at *1101 W Pender St. and 740 W Hastings St. | Budget*

**LA CASA GELATO** (133 D5) (𝒟 E14)

For ice cream lovers, is a real treat with **INSIDER TIP** 216 ice cream flavours to choose from! How about trying the Basil Sesame or the Vodka Lime? To the east of the city centre in an industrial area, so you need to get there by car. *1033 Venables St. | www.lacasagelato.com*

**EDIBLE CANADA** ☺ (U B65) (𝒟 b5)

Trendy organic bistro with terrace and shop. Delicious fish tacos from their street stall and if you arrive in an electric car, there is a charging station right outside the door. *1596 Johnston St. | Granville Island | tel. 604 6 82 66 81 | www.edible canada.com | Moderate*

**HAMBURGER MARY'S** (U B4) (𝒟 b4)

Cosy retro style coffee shop located in the trendy district of Westend. Their breakfasts are also good. *1202 Davie St. | tel. 604 6 87 12 93 | Budget*

**INSIDER TIP KINGYO** (U B2) (𝒟 b2)

Japanese restaurant popular with the young Asian set, serving amazing creations. *871 Denman St. | tel. 604 6 08 16 77 | Moderate*

**MILL MARINE BISTRO A** (U C2) (𝒟 c2)

Ideal for a break, on the new promenade Coal Harbour. *1199 W Cordova St. | tel. 604 6 87 64 55 | Budget–Moderate*

**THE SANDBAR** (U C6) (𝒟 c6)

Excellent fish served in all variations, large bar and **INSIDER TIP** heated rooftop terrace with fireplace, above False Creek. *1535 Johnston St. | Granville Island | tel. 604 6 69 90 30 | Moderate*

## SHOPPING

The main shopping street is the lively *Robson Street*, the large department store, The Bay is north of the Robson Square. *Granville Island* and the *Lonsdale Quay Market* are also popular for their stalls, cafés, and quirky shops.

**FINEST AT SEA SEAFOOD BOUTIQUE** (U B6) (𝒟 b6)

Excellent wild salmon: smoked, frozen, canned and of course the unique *Salmon Candy. 1805 Mast Tower Rd. | Granville Island | www.finestatsea.com*

## ENTERTAINMENT

Listing for current concerts and clubs are in the weekly publication 'Georgia Straight', the monthly magazine 'Where Vancouver', as well as in the weekend edition of the

'Vancouver Sun'. Tickets for concerts, theatre shows, and sporting events are available at *Ticket Master* in the *Vancouver Tourist Info Centre (Waterfront Centre | 200 Burrard St. | tel. 604 2 80 44 44)*. The city centre nightlife is concentrated in the Westend around *Davie* and *Denman St.* as well as in the historic old warehouses of vibrant and trendy *Yaletown*. There is also the popular brew pub *Yaletown Brewing Co.* (U D5) *(₥ d5) (1111 Mainland St., with restaurant)*. On weekends the youth queue up in front of the many clubs on *Granville Street* (U D4) *(₥ d4)*, and meet in the *Commodore Ballroom* (U D4) *(₥ d4)* to enjoy reggae, deep house, funk – with alternating live bands *(868 Granville St.)*.

## WHERE TO STAY

**CENTURY PLAZA** (U C4) *(₥ c4)*
A comfortable mid range hotel within walking distance of Robson Street. The spa is also open to non guests. *236 rooms | 1015 Burrard St. | tel. 604 6 87 05 75 | www.centuryplaza.com | Moderate*

**FAIRMONT WATERFRONT** ☆
(U D3) *(₥ d3)*
Luxury hotel in a prime location between the harbour and Gastown, with beautiful views over the Burrard Inlet. *489 rooms | 900 Canada place Way | tel. 604 6 91 19 91 | www.fairmont.com | Expensive*

**LISTEL VANCOUVER** (U C3) *(₥ c3)*
Stylish, modern hotel in the heart of the city. Good jazz in the restaurant in the evening. *129 rooms | 1300 Robson St. | tel. 604 6 84 84 61 | www.thelistelhotel.com | Moderate–Expensive*

**INSIDER TIP** **SYLVIA** (U A3) *(₥ a3)*
Older, charming mid range hotel in the Westend, right on English Bay beach. *119 rooms | 1154 Gilford St. | tel. 604 6 81 93 21 | www.sylviahotel.com | Budget–Moderate*

## SPORTS & ACTIVITIES

**ECOMARINE PADDLING CENTRE**
(U B5) *(₥ b5)*
Centre for the rental of kayaks and SUP (stand up paddle) boards for customised tours on False Creek, with the scenic backdrop of the city. Courses and guided tours. Rental: C$19–39 for 2 hours. *1668 Duranleau St. | Granville Island | tel. 604 6 89 75 75 | www.ecomarine.com*

# LOW BUDGET

▶ An affordable lunchtime option is Asian cuisine, the area at the western end of *Robson St.*, *Denman St.* and *Davie St.* there are many places where C$6–10 will get you a full tray of sushi and other specialties, such as the simple, but very good, *Samurai Japanese Restaurant (1108 Davie St. | tel. 604 6 09 00 78)*.

▶ The most beautiful views of Vancouver, Burrard Inlet and the harbour will only set you back C$3.75: the cost of the ☆ *SeaBus* ferry ride from Waterfront Station to Lonsdale Quay in north Vancouver. The day ticket (C$9) includes a return and all buses in the city.

▶ *Tickets Tonight* in the *Vancouver Info Centre* sells tickets at half price for performances on the same evening.

▶ On Tuesday between 5pm–9pm the ● *Vancouver Art Gallery* is free of charge, and the excellent *UBC Museum of Anthropology* is only C$9.

## BEACHES

Although the waters of the Pacific Ocean are relatively chilly, even in the summer, the beaches of *English Bay* are nice for a quick dip and some sunbathing. The most beautiful beaches are *Kitsilano* (beach volleyball) and *Jericho* located west of the city centre.

of Hwy. 1, and is today a museum village. The 'inhabitants' of the old trading post guide you through the harsh lifestyle of the trappers in the 19th century. *Daily July/ Aug 9am–5pm, otherwise 10am–5pm | admission C$7.80*

Fort Langley town itself also deserves a stroll. The picturesque main street, Glover

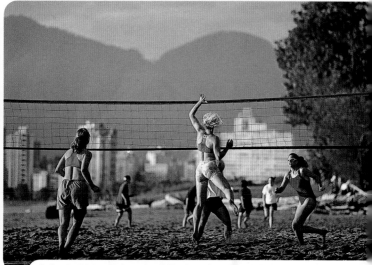

Kitsilano Beach is Vancouver's most beautiful beach, popular not only with beach volleyball enthusiasts

## INFORMATION

### VANCOUVER TOURIST CENTRE
(U D3) (*@ d3*)

Multilingual staff. Accommodation service, tickets, sightseeing tours. *Waterfront Centre | 200 Burrard St. | tel. 604 6 83 20 00 | www.tourismvancouver.com*

## WHERE TO GO

### LANGLEY (133 E5) (*@ E14*)

INSIDER TIP ► *Fort Langley National Historic Site*, the old fur trading fort on the Fraser River, is located approx. 50km/30mi east

Road, is lined with shady trees, numerous antique shops, boutiques and pleasant restaurants such as the *Lamplighter Café*. *9213 Glover Rd | tel. 604 8 88 64 64 | Moderate*

### RICHMOND (133 D5) (*@ E14*)

About half an hour south of the city centre (you can also take the *Canada Line metro rail*) is Vancouver's Chinese neighbourhood. Innumerable Asian restaurants line No. 3 Road, and near by, on the banks of the Fraser River, is the distinctive *Richmond Oval*, venue of the Olympic speed skating events.

# VANCOUVER ISLAND

Vancouver Island is the largest (450km/ 280mi) island on the west coast of North America and it is a world in its own. A fascinating primeval landscape of deep fjords and high mountains, laced with peaceful bays and spectacular beaches. The island's rewards are in its contrasts: sleepy fishing villages, Native American reserves and lumberjack camps in the isolated north, bustling holiday villages and the elegant capital Victoria in the south. But above all, the island is ideal for a holiday in and with nature.

To date only one road leads along the whole island, Highway 19, the north-south thoroughfare. For the majority of the distance it runs along on the eastern coast, protected by a long stretch of mountain massif. The wild, rainy western coast – home to the Pacific Rim National Park with its unique rainforests and rugged rocks – is still almost inaccessible and thus an ideal destination for wilderness hikers and kayakers. The mild eastern coast, however, is very accessible and is known for its bathing beaches – the shallow waters of the Strait of Georgia, which separates the island from the Mainland, are pleasantly warm in the summer. Island information: *Tourism Vancouver Island | Information Centre on Hwy. 4 at Tofino | tel. 250 7 54 35 00 | www.vancouverisland.travel*

Photo: Orca breaching off Vancouver Island

Whales and rainforests, unspoilt beaches and verdant fjords – these are the many and varied charms of the west coast

# CAMPBELL RIVER

(132 C5) (*M D14*) **Passionate anglers' eyes light up when they hear the name of this port city (population 31,000) one of the largest cities on Vancouver Island.**

Every summer the largest salmon in Canada are caught here, in the central part of the island. King Salmon weighing 30kg/66lbs are not uncommon. In high season the waters off the town are full of boats. *Quadra Island,* a barrier island that can be reached by ferry, is a Kwakiutl Indian reserve. This is also where you will find the INSIDER TIP *Nuyumbalees Cultural Centre (in summer, daily 10am–5pm |*

Cowichan totem poles in Duncan

*(3 rooms | 492 South Island Hwy. | tel. 250 9 23 28 48 | www.heronslandinghotel. com | Budget–Moderate).*

### WHERE TO GO

### STRATHCONA PROV. PARK
### (132 C5) (*ᗰ D14*)

The oldest provincial park in British Columbia, 50km/30mi west of Campbell River, is especially interesting for hikers. It has a well developed network of paths leading from the two roads in the park up into the alpine regions. *Golden Hinde* is the highest mountain at 2500m/8200ft. Especially beautiful is the hike to *Flower Ridge* at the southern end of the *Buttle Lake.* On the banks of the Upper Campbell Lake is the cosy *Strathcona Park Lodge* which offers hiking, mountaineering and canoeing. *46 rooms, holiday homes and chalets | tel. 250 2 86 31 22 | www.strath cona.bc.ca | Moderate*

# DUNCAN

**(133 D6) (*ᗰ D15*) The town (pop. 5000) in the fertile Cowichan Valley was not particularly special, until the Cowichan Indians on the adjacent reserve founded a cultural centre to honour their traditions and began to carve totem poles.** Everywhere in the village you will now see brightly painted poles – widely appreciated by the locals in the town as they attraction tourists and bring in money.

### SIGHTSEEING

### BC FOREST DISCOVERY CENTRE

Everything to do with logging and lumberjacks – from old chain saws, to a sawmill to a lumberjack camp – can all be explore in this open-air museum. *Daily in the summer 10am–4pm | admission C$15 and*

*admission C$10 | Cape Mudge), a true treasure trove of Native American masks of the Kwakiutl. If you would to overnight the try the Tsa-Kwa-Luten Lodge (35 rooms | Quadra Island | tel. 250 2 85 20 42 | www.capemudgeresort.bc.ca | Moderate– Expensive)* a lodge (with campsite) run by Native Americans and decorated with carvings. Another option is a modern, small hotel with sea views and good location close to the harbour ☆ *Heron's Landing*

includes a ride on an old steam train | *northern edge of town, Hwy. 1 | www. bcforestmuseum.com*

### QUW'UTSU 'UTSUN' CULTURAL CENTRE
Large cultural centre of the Cowichan Indians with dance performances and a café serving Native American cuisine. *In the summer daily 10am–5pm | admission C$1 | 200 Cowichan Way*

## FOOD & DRINK

### INSIDER TIP GENOA BAY CAFÉ
Somewhat out of the way on a secluded and idyllic bay, but the trip is well worth it. *5000 Genoa Bay Rd. | tel. 250 7 46 76 21 | Moderate*

## WHERE TO GO

### PORT RENFREW (133 D6) (*∅ D15*)
From Duncan the recently opened and paved Hwy. 18 leads 150km/93m via Lake Cowichan and densely forested mountains to Port Renfrew on the west coast. The small, secluded village lies on the southern edge of the *Pacific Rim National Park* (the starting point for the West Coast trail) and offers a long beach and camping in the adjacent Native American reserve. The INSIDER TIP *Botanical Beach* with bizarre rock formations and diverse marine in large tidal pools (first check when the tide is low). Continue on Hwy. 14 from Port Renfrew to Victoria and you will have done a roundtrip of the south of Vancouver Island.

# NANAIMO

(133 D5) (*∅ D14*) **Nanaimo is the northern ferry port for the ships to the mainland and a good starting point for tours to the central part of the island.**

The attractive town (pop. 70,000) is the second largest on Vancouver Island, with sparkling yacht marinas, a lovely harbour promenade and numerous coastal parks. In recent years the town has become a dive destination. Its several shipwrecks, clear visibility and diverse marine life all attract divers.

## SPORTS & ACTIVITIES

### WILDPLAY ELEMENT PARK
Adventure park for both adults and children: bungee jumps, zip lining, rope climbing section – all with plenty of adrenaline. *Prices from C$40 | 35 Nanaimo River Rd. | tel. 250 7 16 78 74 | www.wildplay.com*

## WHERE TO STAY

### BUCCANEER INN ☺
Comfortable eco-motel (recycled paper, waste separation) near the ferry from the mainland. Good base for divers. *14 rooms |*

---

⭐ **Pacific Rim National Park**
Ancient trees, rainforests and wild, pristine beaches along the west coast → p. 44

⭐ **Inside Passage**
Silent fjords, deep blue water: the most beautiful coast in all of Canada → p. 46

⭐ **Stubbs Island Whale Watching**
See the pods of magnificent killer whales → p. 46

⭐ **Victoria Inner Harbour**
Hustle and bustle, yachts and large flower pots hanging from the street lamps → p. 48

**MARCO POLO HIGHLIGHTS**

*1577 Stewart Ave. | tel. 250 7 53 12 46 |*
*Moderate*

## WHERE TO GO

### GULF ISLANDS
(132–133 C–D4–6) (*𝄞 D–E 14–15*)
A whole archipelago of small islands lies between Vancouver Island and the mainland. *Saltspring*, *Galiano* and *Gabriola* they are the most important – they are accessible by ferry from Swartz Bay, Crofton

The Pacific Rim National Park is one of 42 national parks in Canada

or Nanaimo. The climate here is particularly mild and sunny – even palm trees grow in some places! Laid back artists, writers and artisans have chosen to settle here. The best way to explore the islands is by bicycle: you can travel quickly from island to island by ferry and on some of the islets – where certain parts are car free – a bicycle is the best means of transport.

### PARKSVILLE (133 D5) (*𝄞 D14*)
The charm of Nanaimo lies in the surrounding area: around 25km/15mi to the north, around Parksville and *Qualicum Beach* there are some very attractive beaches with warm waters. A 20 minute drive inland on Hwy. 4 leads to the *MacMillan Provincial Park* where you can marvel at the 800 year old Douglas firs and cedar trees, or the cascades of *Little Qualicum Falls* (hiking trails). You can then stay the night at *Tigh-Na-Mara Resort (192 rooms | 1155 Resort Drive | tel. 250 2 48 20 72 | www.tigh-na-mara.com | Moderate–Expensive)* with log cabins and apartments right on the beach and a large spa with mineral pool and 🌀 seaweed, clay and sea salt organic wraps.

# PACIFIC RIM NAT. PARK

(132–133 C–D 5–6) (*𝄞 D14–15*) ★ ●
**The wildest and most beautiful sections of the coast form part of this 150 square mile nature reserve. The park protects an ancient rainforest, rugged cliffs and driftwood-strewn beaches, such as the 11km/7mi aptly named *Long Beach*.**
In the *Kwisitis Centre* at ⭐ *Wickaninnish Beach* gives a very detailed and competent explanation of the natural history of the region. The friendly rangers are also on hand to give you tips for hikes. The nature trails are particularly impressive, such as the *Rainforest Trail*, and given the weather conditions in the area it is a good idea to equip yourself with a waterproof cape. The small archipelago of the *Broken Group Islands* is a great destination for wilderness kayakers, and if the weather conditions are

good then hikers should book the week-long *West Coast Trail* (75km/47mi long and reservation required, *tel. 250 7 26 44 53*) from Port Renfrew to Bamfield. Highly recommended is also the ● *Wild Pacific Trail* in the southern town of *Ucluelet*, which stretches over three sections of the rugged coast. From *Tofino*, the small port city on the northern edge of the park, you can take boat trips to secluded coves and go whale watching in the *Clayoquot Sound*. It is also very popular to go **INSIDER TIP** bear watching from a boat, a safe way to observe the predators.

## SPORTS & ACTIVITIES

### ATLEO RIVER AIR SERVICE
Organised tours by seaplane over glaciers, fjords and waterfalls. *50 Wingen Lane | tel. 866 6 62 85 36 | www.atleoair.com*

### BARKLEY SOUND SERVICE
A former Norwegian freight ferry offers cruises in the Barkley Sound. Full day trips from Port Alberni to Ucluelet and Bamfield. They also transport hikers to the *West Coast Trail* and kayakers to the *Broken Group Islands* (book in advance). *Port Alberni | tel. 250 7 23 83 13 | www.ladyrosemarine. com*

### REMOTE PASSAGES
Motorboat and rubber dingy trips to observe grey whales, orca and bears and to the hot springs on a secluded island. *51 Wharf St. | tel. 250 7 25 33 30 | www. remotepassages.com*

### SURF SISTER
Ride a wave for an exciting adrenaline rush: in spite of the name they offer both women-only and mixed courses. A trial course, including board and wetsuit, costs C$75. *625 Campbell St. | tel. 250 7 25 44 56 | www.surfsister.com*

## FOOD & DRINK

### NORWOODS ☺
Creative west coast cuisine in a cosy interior styled with lots of wood. The ingredients, such as mussels or Dungeness crab, are supplied by local fishermen, who rely on sustainable catch. *1714 Peninsula Rd. | Ucluelet | tel. 250 7 26 70 01 | Moderate– Expensive*

### SHELTER
Try the salmon and halibut in a Macadamia crust, or the pork chops in apple sauce. Very good: Dungeness crab, fresh from the west coast. *601 Campbell St. | tel. 250 7 25 33 53 | Moderate*

### SOBO
Delicious, very healthy west coast cuisine. The lunchtime menu is very reasonably priced. *311 Neill St. | tel. 250 7 25 23 41 | Expensive*

## WHERE TO STAY

### HETINKIS LODGE
Three luxurious apartments in a wonderful location on a rock fringed bay. *Ucluelet | tel. 250 7 26 29 28 | www.hetinkislodge. com | Moderate–Expensive*

### **INSIDER TIP** LONG BEACH LODGE ✦
Your own chic lodge right on the beach, with surf school and good restaurant. Many of the rooms overlook the sea. Ideal for families. *41 rooms, 20 cottages | 1441 Pacific Rim Hwy. | tel. 250 7 25 24 42 | www.long beachlodgeresort.com | Expensive*

### WHALERS ON THE POINT GUESTHOUSE ✦
Cosy hostel in the centre of the village, the ideal base for surfers, backpackers and active vacationers. *4–6 bed dorm rooms and 4 double rooms | 81 West St. Tofino |*

# PORT HARDY

**(132 C4)** *(ØJ C13)* **The busy port is evidence that the town (pop. 4000), in the wild north of Vancouver Island, is an important fishing base.**

For visitors, Port Hardy is the starting point for the *Inside Passage* and rewarding trips: you can see whales, bears and eagles on kayak, hikes, flights and boat trips.

## WHERE TO STAY

### GLEN LYON INN 〰

Comfortable hotel with beautiful harbour views and if you are lucky you may spot a bald eagle from your window. Good in-house pub/restaurant. *6435 Hardy Bay Rd. | tel. 250 9 49 71 15 | www.glenlyoninn. com | Budget–Moderate*

### INSIDER TIP GREAT BEAR LODGE

A floating eco lodge that is the base for grizzly bear and nature observation tours. Great location in a fjord on the mainland coast. Access is by seaplane from Port Hardy. *Tel. 250 9 49 94 96 | www.great beartours.com | Moderate–Expensive*

## WHERE TO GO

### ALERT BAY (132 C4) *(ØJ C13)*

The village (pop. 600) on a small offshore island around 40km/25mi south on the Hwy. 19 (ferry from port McNeill) is home to the Kwakwaka'wakw Indians *(Kwakiutl)*, famous for their particularly expressive carving. The most beautiful heirlooms of the tribe – old masks, decorated chests and totem poles – are exhibited in the INSIDER TIP *U' Mista Cultural Centre (summer daily 9am–5pm, otherwise only Tue–*

Sat | Admission C$11.20, guided tours organised by the Culture Shock Gallery on the ferry port *(tel. 250 9 74 24 84 | www. cultureshockgallery.ca)*. For some a night right on the water try the *Seine Boat Inn (10 rooms | www.seineboatinn.com) Budget–Moderate*

### INSIDE PASSAGE ★ ● 〰 (132 B–C 2–4) *(ØJ D–E 13–15)*

The 500km/310mi long coastal shipping route runs along the west coast, and was once the route followed by thousands of adventurers on their way to the gold fields of Klondike and to Alaska. There are still no roads along the coast, which is lined by numerous fjords. The only way to experience the legendary route is by cruise ship (from Vancouver) or on one of the *BC Ferries* on a 15 hour trip between *Port Hardy* and *Prince Rupert* (you will need to book several months in advance, information on site at *tel. 888 2 23 37 79, www.bcferries.com)*.

### TELEGRAPH COVE (132 C4) *(ØJ C13)*

The former fishing hamlet (pop. 20), less than an hour's drive south of Port Hardy, is now a Mecca for whale watchers and researchers. Several groups of orca live here in the salmon-rich waters of a marine reserve (between the mainland and Vancouver Island) and they can be seen here throughout the summer. Half day boat tours are on offer between May to October by ★ 〰 *Stubbs Island Whale Watching,* they travel out to the Johnstone Strait, a marine reserve for orca *(Telegraph Cove | ticket C$84 | tel. 800 6 65 30 66 | www.stubbsisland.com)*. At the junction to Telegraph Cove on Hwy. 19, the Canadian lumber industry cultivates its image with the *North Island Discovery Centre* that offers free guided tours of sawmills, logging camps and areas of impact *(by prior arrangement: tel. 250 9 56 38 44)*.

**CITY** **WHERE TO START?**
**Inner Harbour** is the heart of the city; from here it is only a short walk to the Royal British Columbia Museum and to Parliament in the south and – in the north – to the old town on Government Street and Chinatown on Fisgard Street. Public parking is just north of Inner Harbour along Wharf Street

# VICTORIA

**(133 D6) (*☐ E15*) The capital city of British Columbia (pop. 345,000) basks in the colonial legacy of the British Empire – with landscaped gardens, Victorian architecture, double-decker buses and horse-drawn carriages for sightseeing.**

A stylish English tea in the ivy-covered Fairmont Empress Hotel (a landmark dating from 1906) is a tradition in the city.

The mild climate (ideal for g────asts) and its location on the w─────of the Juan de Fuca Strait make Victoria one of the most popular resorts in the west. Victoria has been the capital of British Columbia since 1871; it was only founded 30 years prior to that as a trading post for the Hudson's Bay Company. It is now popular with well-heeled seniors who want to spend their retirement playing golf or a enjoying the extensive *Butchard Gardens* at the northern end of the city. It is also popular with young people who enjoy sailing and who appreciate the leisure activities of the city.

## SIGHTSEEING

### BEACON HILL PARK

The urban park is the site of the 'Mile 0' plaque (intersection of Douglas and Dallas Rd) that marks the start of the *Trans-Canada Highway* which runs 8000km/ 5000mi east to Newfoundland. From here you can take the a *Scenic Marine*

Inside Passage: legendary waterway through the islands off the west coast of British Columbia

Inner Harbour Victoria: a vibrant meeting place no matter what season or time of day

*Drive* that follows the coast through beautiful suburbs such as Oak Bay.

### INNER HARBOUR ★
No visit to Victoria is complete without a walk along the harbour basin, filled with sailboats and yachts, to some of the city's major attractions. On the eastern side is the famed *Fairmont Empress Hotel,* on the northern side is the old town with its shopping streets and small alleys, while to the south, in a commanding position, are the magnificent Parliament buildings dating from 1898, with a statue of Queen Victoria. The best way to explore the harbour, is to take a trip on one of the small *Harbour Ferry Company boats (roundtrip C$22 | departure from Empress Hotel | victoriaharbourferry.com).*

### ROYAL BRITISH COLUMBIA MUSEUM
The largest museum in the province; the natural history section includes a micro rainforest, a tidal pool and the cultural section has magnificent totem poles and exhibitions about pioneer history. With IMAX cinema and shop. *Daily 10am–5pm |* *admission C$17, with IMAX C$24 | 675 Belleville St.*

## TOURS

### ORCA SPIRIT ADVENTURES ●
Summer whale watching trips (in either a zodiac or a covered boat) to the islands off the coast where several pods of orca live. *3 hour tour C$9 | Inner Harbour | departure outside the Empress Hotel | tel. 888 6 72 67 22 | www.whalewatching adventure.com*

## FOOD & DRINK

### FLYING OTTER GRILL ☃
Popular pub with a terrace on the harbour, surrounded by yachts and seaplanes; good for breakfast, lunch and dinner. *950 Wharf St. | tel. 250 4 14 42 20 | Moderate*

### INSIDER TIP MO:LÉ ☺
A cosy coffee shop offering tasty multicultural cuisine, organic ingredients are used extensively. Only open for breakfast and

lunch. *554 Pandora Ave. | tel. 250 3 85 66 53 | Budget–Moderate*

### SWAN'S PUB AND CAFE

A popular pub in the city, serving salads and fresh fish, that is also a good option for an evening out. *506 Pandora St. | tel. 250 3 61 33 10 | Budget*

## SHOPPING

### MARKET SQUARE

The brick buildings of the beautifully reno-vated warehouses at the harbour are full of shops, art galleries and restaurants. *560 Johnson St.*

## WHERE TO STAY

### FAIRMONT EMPRESS

Steeped in traditional, but recently reno-vated. *477 rooms | 721 Government St. | tel. 250 3 84 81 11 | www.fairmont.com | Expensive*

### QUEEN VICTORIA HOTEL

Modern tower block hotel, centrally locat-ed. *146 rooms | 655 Douglas St. | tel. 250 3 86 13 12 | www.qvhotel.com | Moderate*

## INFORMATION

### TOURISM VICTORIA

Information Office at Inner Harbour, they also help with accommodation. *812 Wharf St. | tel. 250 9 53 20 33 | www.tourism victoria.com*

## WHERE TO GO

### FISGARD LIGHTHOUSE

(133 D6) (*E15*)

Ever since 1860 the picturesque light-house – the oldest in the Canadian west coast – has been guiding vessels into the harbour. It lies 15km/9mi further west of Victoria on the Hwy. 1. From the light-house the highway continues westward to a real gourmet treat: ☀ *Sooke Harbour House (1528 Whiffen Spit Rd. | Sooke | tel. 250 6 42 34 21 | www.sookeharbourhouse. com | Moderate–Expensive, also 28 rooms | Expensive)*, perfectly positioned above a small bay and serving delicious regional cuisine.

### INSIDER TIP SHAW OCEAN DISCOVERY CENTRE (133 D6) (*E15*)

The underwater ecosystem of Canada's west coast of is the subject of this excel-lent, non-profit aquarium, half an hour's drive north of Victoria. *Daily 10am–4pm | admission C$14 | 9811 Seaport Place | Sidney*

# LOW BUDGET

▶ Ideal base for low budget tours to Vancouver Island is the *Painted Turtle Guest House (20 rooms | 121 Bastion St. | Nanaimo | tel. 866 3 09 44 32 | www.paintedturtle.ca)* in Nanaimo. The pleasantly restored building in the old town is an in-formal forum of information about lifts and tours. A night in one of the dorms costs C$25; single rooms start at C$73.

▶ A wilderness lodge on a secluded fjord need not be extremely ex-pensive. On *Quadra Island* the ecologically run ☺ *Discovery Islands Lodge (8 beds | Surge narrows | tel. 250 2 85 28 23 | www.discovery-islands-lodge.com)* offers a double room incl. breakfast for C$96. Bring your own sleeping bag. Full day kayak tours cost C$99.

# BRITISH COLUMBIA

British Columbia (in daily use abbreviated to BC) boastfully calls itself the most scenic province in Canada. And not without cause: the westernmost region offers the largest variety of landscapes and the best opportunities for an adventurous holiday. Whether canoeing, hiking, heli-skiing, fishing, biking or white water rafting: BC has thrills and adventure to suit for every taste. The province even has sunny beaches and waters warm enough for swimming – such as the popular beaches of Okanagan Lake. The mainland of this large province covers 365,000 square miles province – a broad field of possibilities just waiting to be explored. The offshore island of

Vancouver Island *(→ p. 40)* as well as the city of Vancouver *(→ p. 32)* both deserve their own chapter. The entire region is characterised by large mountain ranges – not only from the Rockies, because they only start on the extreme eastern edge of the province – but numerous other large mountain ranges that all form part of the North American Cordillera. Verdant mountains alternate with high plateaus into which rivers – such as the Fraser River – have cut broad valleys. Only the extreme north–east, the region around Dawson Creek, is flat. There, the province extends to the foothills of the prairie. And on the border with the United States at Osoyoos,

Photo: Horseback riding in the Chilcotin region

Between the Rockies and the Pacific: towering mountains, jewel-like lakes, fascinating pioneer towns – British Columbia has it all

you will find Canada's only desert – one that even includes cacti and rattlesnakes.

# CARIBOO REGION

(133 D–E 3–4) (*EF 12–14*) **The steppe-like plateau on the upper reaches of the**

**Fraser River is Canada's own Wild West: hilly ranch country with large herds of cattle and gold rush towns.**

In order to supply the miners during the great gold rush of 1860, the *Cariboo Wagon Road* was built, the first road in western Canada. Highway 97 follows the old route from the south and opens up the region. Today, many of the small ranch villages (first set up as stagecoach stations) were named after the distances from the original start of the road in *Lillooet (133 E4) (☐ E13)*: *70 Mile House, 100 Mile House* etc. The main town and starting point for tours around *Barkerville, Likely* or *Horsefly* is *Williams Lake (133 E3) (☐ E13)*, which hosts a rodeo every 1st of July.

**COTTONWOOD HOUSE**
**(133 E3) (☐ E12)**
A historic site in Cottonwood, a faithfully restored coach inn dating back to 1864, also horse-drawn carriage rides. *Daily in the summer 10am–5pm | admission C$5 | on Hwy. 26*

Where many holiday dreams becomes reality: Clearwater Lake Lodge

## SIGHTSEEING

**BARKERVILLE**
**(133 E3) (☐ F12)**
During the gold rush days in 1870 Barkerville was the largest city north of San Francisco. Today it is a INSIDER TIP wonderfully nostalgic museum village with Wild West facades, wooden sidewalks and actors who enact the pioneering lifestyle. Even the restaurants are worth a visit: the historic *Wake–Up Jake Café (tel. 250 9 94 32 59 | Budget)* with its hearty gold rush food, or the *Lung Duck Tong Restaurant* that serves good Chinese food *(tel. 250 9 94 34 58 | Budget)*. *Visitor Centre and museum daily 8.30am–8pm | admission in summer C$14 | at the town entrance on Hwy. 26*

**WELLS (133 E3) (☐ F12)**
The old mining town on the western edge of the Cariboo Mountains has evolved today into an arts centre for the young, creative and environmentally conscious, with galleries and theatres. In the summer can even make pottery or do an art course, such as at *Beck's Pottery (www.beckspottery.com)* or at *Island Mountain Arts (www.imarts.com)*.

## WHERE TO STAY

**BECKER'S LODGE**
Lodge right on the lake, also chalets and camping. Equipment and rental for the week-long canoe trips on the Bowron Lakes. *10 rooms | Wells | tel. 250 9 92 88 64 | www.beckerslodge.ca | Moderate*

### ECO TOURS BC & THE LODGE
Simple wilderness lodge deep in the hinterland of the Cariboo Mountains, an hour's drive east of Williams Lake. Also ⏱ INSIDERTIP Grizzly bear watching tours, done within nature conservation rules. *6 rooms | Likely | tel. 250 7 90 22 92 | ecotours-bc.com/the-lodge | Moderate*

### KOKANEE BAY MOTEL ≈
Simple motel overlooking the lake, also log cabins and a camping site right on the shore. *3728 Hwy. 9 | Lac La Hache | tel. 250 3 96 73 45 | www.kokaneebaycariboo. com | Budget*

### WELLS HOTEL
Historic country inn in the gold rush country around Barkerville, with restaurant and bar. *13 rooms | Wells | tel. 250 9 94 34 27 | www.wellshotel.com | Budget–Moderate*

## INFORMATION

### CARIBOO CHILCOTIN COAST TOURISM ASSOCIATION
*204350 Barnard St. | Williams Lake | tel. 250 3 92 22 26 | www.landwithoutlimits.com*

## WHERE TO GO

### CHILCOTIN REGION
(132–133 C–D3) (*D–E12*)
If, from Williams Lake, you still want to go deeper into the wilderness, then you should take a trip into the backcountry on the Highway 20. It leads 450km/280mi further west through the ranch region of Chilcotin and the massive *Tweedsmuir Provincial Park* (campsites, trails) up to the coast at *Bella Coola* – a perfect destination for anglers and wilderness hikers. Not far from here is where Alexander MacKenzie reached the Pacific in 1793 – Canada's first transcontinental crossing. In summer *BC Ferries* do the crossing from Bella Coola to Port Hardy three times a week, which makes a roundtrip back to the south possible *(reservations recommended: tel. 888 2 23 37 79 | www.bcferries.com)*. A good overnight option are the cosy, rustic log cabins of INSIDERTIP *Clearwater Lake Lodge (7 rooms | Hwy. 20 | Marshall Kleene | tel. 250 4 76 11 50 | www.clearwaterlakelodge.com | Moderate)*. And there is also the historic ⏱ *Tweedsmuir Park Lodge (Hwy. 20 | Tweedsmuir Park | tel. 877 9 82 24 07 | www.tweedsmuirparklodge.com | Expensive)* with ten luxurious log cabins that is now run as an eco resort.

# DAWSON CREEK

(133 E1) (*F10*) **Dawson Creek (pop. 11,000)** would have been an inconspic-

uous farming village had it not been for *Milestone 0* on the main road in the town centre. This is where the famous *Alaska Highway* begins.

Now fully paved, the road covers almost 2300km/1430mi to Delta Junction, Alaska. Exhibit in the visitor centre and the *Walter Wright Pioneer Village* illustrate the history of the region. The painstaking construction of the highway by American troops in World War II is illustrated in the *Alaska Highway House (admission free |*

At 1327m/4354ft on  *Rogers Pass* a memorial commemorates the completion of the *Trans-Canada Highway* 1962. In the visitor centre next to it there are tips for hiking routes – beware, it often rains along the western flank of the mountains! The exhibits in the visitor centre clearly explain the painstaking construction of railway 100 years ago. Accommodations and restaurants are in the old railway village of *Golden* (pop. 4100) at the eastern entrance to the park.

The Trans-Canada Highway climbs to a height of 1327m/4354ft at Rogers Pass

*10201 10 St.).* The *Inn on the Creek (48 rooms | 10600 8th St. | tel. 250 7 82 81 36 | Budget–Moderate)* is a comfortable motel at the southern entrance to the town.

# GLACIER NAT. PARK

**(134 B5) (*⌀ H–J15*) Numerous black and grizzly bears live in the 520 square miles reserve in the glacier capped Selkirk Mountains, Hwy. 1 winds for miles through various passes in the park.**

## SIGHTSEEING & TOURS

**INSIDER TIP ▶ NORTHERN LIGHTS WOLF CENTRE**
Privately run conservation centre with an enclosure with a pack of grey wolves, which you can view here at close quarters. *Daily in summer 9am–7pm | admission C$12 | 1745 Short Rd. | Golden*

### GLACIER RAFT COMPANY
Half and full day rafting trips with sturdy rubber boats on the Kicking Horse River. *612 N 7th St. | Golden | tel. 250 3 44 65 21 | www.glacierraft.com*

### COLUMBIA VALLEY B & B
Eco-friendly, European style B & B with a dining room (for overnight guests only) serving traditional Austrian and Canadian dishes. *5 rooms | 2304 Hwy. 95 | Golden | tel. 250 3 48 25 08 | www.columbiavalley bnb.com | Budget*

### GOLDENWOOD LODGE ☼
Located just outside of town, this tranquil retreat is a modern B & B with accommodation in wooden cottages, tepees or in the main lodge. *13 rooms | 2493 Holmes Deakin Rd. | Golden | tel. 250 3 44 76 85 | www.goldenwoodlodge.com | Budget–Moderate*

# KAMLOOPS

**(133 E–F4) (🛧 F14) The third largest city in the province (pop. 86,000) is not that impressive but it does lie at the crossroads of the major highways and, as it has some large shopping malls, it is a good place to stock up on supplies before a trip into the hinterland.**

The centrally located *Victoria Street* has undergone a revival in recent years and many restaurants and small shops are worth a browse.

## SIGHTSEEING

### SECWEPEMC NATIVE HERITAGE CENTRE
A museum and heritage park that illustrates the rich history, language and culture of the Shuswap Indians through storytelling with dance and music performances. *Daily in the summer 8am–4pm, otherwise Sat/Sun closed | admission C$12 | 355 Yellowhead Hwy.*

## FOOD & DRINK

### COMMODORE GRAND
Restaurant and entertainment venue for the younger crowd in the old town. Good salads, steaks and pizza. Live music after 10pm. *369 Victoria St. | tel. 250 8 51 31 00 | Budget–Moderate*

### RIC'S GRILL
Good steaks, ribs, salmon – a trendy old town eatery. *227 Victoria St. | tel. 250 3 72 77 71 | Moderate*

# HUDSON'S BAY COMPANY

Hats made of Canadian beaver felt, especially hop hats and tricorns were very fashionable in the 17th and 18th century and demand meant that trappers and fur traders moved westwards into the new continent. Big profits were to be made from the soft under fur of the beaver, as its structure matted well into felt. *Hudson's Bay Company* was founded in 1670 and the fur trading company went on to become one of the largest commercial empires. The English King Charles II gave the company trading rights for all the lands in the drainage basin of Hudson Bay and the company's trading area eventually covered one twelfth of the earth's surface. Their forts later became towns and their trade routes became highways.

Crossing the Fraser River gorge by gondola

RIVER COUNTRY INN

## RIVER COUNTRY INN

Good, clean motel is situated on the river, well away from the noise of the Trans-Canada Highway. *58 rooms | 1530 River St. | tel. 250 3 74 15 30 | www.riverlandinn. kamloops.com | Budget–Moderate*

## WHERE TO GO

### INSIDER TIP ADAMS RIVER
(133 F4) (*ω F13*)

All along the west coast, the salmon swim upstream to spawn and you can experience a spectacular salmon run in early October in the Adams River, about 70km/ 43mi north-east of Kamloops. Several hundreds of thousands of bright red sock-eye salmon jostle water that is only knee-deep. Every fourth year is a peak year: within a period of two weeks of more than 2 million salmon come to spawn and die – the next peak is 2014.

### LYTTON (133 E5) (*ω E14*)

The tiny village (pop. 400) 150km/93mi south-west of Kamloops, at the confluence of the Thompson River and Fraser River, is a INSIDER TIP popular starting point for white water rafting trips. South of the town is the impressive 🌿 gorge where the Fraser River starts on its 100km/62mi journey through the Coast Mountains. At *Hell's Gate,* the narrowest part of the gorge, about 50km/30mi south of Lytton, a 🌿 gondola goes down to the riverbank, where you can watch salmon in the summer, fight their way upstream through the whirlpools. *Kumsheen Rafting Adventures (on Hwy. 1 | tel. 250 4 55 22 96 or tel. 800 6 63 66 67 | www.kumsheen.com)* offers rafting on the Thompson and Fraser rivers. A good place to relax in style for a few days is the ● *Echo Valley Ranch (Jesmond | tel. 250 4 59 23 86 | www.evranch.com | full board Expensive)* to the north, they also have a Thai spa and horseback riding.

## SHOPPING

### ABERDEEN MALL

You can shop for hours in this huge shopping mall on the west side of the city. Good shops are The Bay, SportChek and Roots Canada. *1320 West Trans-Canada Hwy.*

## WHERE TO STAY

### PLAZA HOTEL

Historic cattle baron hotel that has been lovingly renovated with lots of attention to detail, in the heart of the city, and with a restaurant. *6 rooms | 405 Victoria St. | tel. 250 3 77 80 75 | www.plazaheritagehotel. com | Moderate*

**SHUSWAP LAKES** (133 F4) *(m F–G14)*
The large lake actually has four bodies of water; it is an hour's drive east of Kamloops and is a popular recreation area for water sports enthusiasts. Shuswap Lake itself has a more than 600 miles of deserted and densely forested shoreline. In the small villages such as *Salmon Arm* or *Sicamous* you can rent a houseboat and explore the labyrinth of creeks and coves in peace *(Twin Anchors Houseboat Vacations | 750 Marine Park Dr. | Salmon Arm | tel. 250 8 32 27 45 | www.twinanchors.com)*. Overnight tip for golf fans: the idyllically situated *Inn at the Ninth Hole (5091 20 Ave. SE | Salmon Arm | tel. 250 8 33 01 85 | www.ninthhol. com | Moderate)*.

# REVELSTOKE

(134 B4–5) *(m G13)* **From July to early September the ★ wild flower meadows on Mount Revelstoke, high above the** railroad town (pop. 8500) – an unforgettable sight. About 100 wild flower species grow around the summit.

In the village you will find restaurants, hotels and campsites. Access to Revelstoke National Park is easy: a gravel road leads to the 1938m/6358 high *Mount Revelstoke* (in midsummer a shuttle bus is available). At the summit there are some lovely, short hiking trails while down below in the valley the INSIDER TIP *Giant Cedars Trail* – which leads from the Trans-Canada Highway through dense forests of centuries-old cedars and Douglas fir trees – is also worth a hike.

## SIGHTSEEING

### REVELSTOKE DAM VISITOR CENTRE
The modern visitor centre at the northern end of the village explains the role of the dam on the Columbia River. Those interested in technical things can travel a further 150km/93mi upstream to the mighty

Evening in Revelstoke, a popular holiday resort and starting point for mountain hikes

*Mica Dam (Wed–Mon 10am–4 pm | guides C$6 | info tel. 250 8 14 66 97).*

## REVELSTOKE RAILWAY MUSEUM

The showpiece of the museum is one of the largest steam locomotives to run in Canada. *Daily in summer 9am–6pm, otherwise Thu–Sun 11am–4 pm | admission C$10 | 719 Track St.*

### WHERE TO STAY

**GLACIER HOUSE RESORT** ☼☀
Modern log cabin lodge with views of the mountains, just outside town near the Revelstoke Dam. *26 rooms | 1870 Glacier Lane | tel. 250 8 37 95 94 | www.glacier house.com | Budget–Moderate*

### WHERE TO GO

**ARROW LAKES (134 B5–6) ($\textit{Ⓜ}$ G13)**
Revelstoke is located at the northern end of the elongated chain of lakes on the Columbia River. On the Highways 23 and 6 you can explore the largely unpopulated region and historic towns like *Kaslo*, hot springs such as **INSIDER TIP** *Nakusp Hot Springs* and ghost towns like *Sandon*. Car ferries service the towns along the lake shore.

# OKANAGAN VALLEY

**(134 B5–6) ($\textit{Ⓜ}$ F14–15) The valley is defined by an elongated chain of lakes, and due to its warm summers and mild climate, it has developed into an orchard and wine area, one that is also a popular recreation and holiday spot.**

The southern end of the valley is extremely dry, even cacti grow there but the slopes around the lakes burst into a blaze of glory in spring, when the apple, cherry and peach trees blossom. In summer and autumn you can buy honey, jam, cider, and of course fresh fruit at roadside stalls. The wineries that are scattered throughout the whole valley today produce some excellent wines – after more than 40 years of experimentation – and are well worth

# CANADA'S WINE COUNTRY

Fifty years ago, wine was of very little interest to Canadians. Everyone drank ale, stout and Guinness, western Canada was beer drinking country. However, the success of California's Napa Valley and other wine regions in Oregon and Washington allowed the Canadians to follow suit. The conditions in the Okanagan Valley are well suited to vineyards: sandy soil, hot, dry summers. Even ice wine (wine from grapes frozen on the vine) does very well here, as winter usually arrives quite abruptly

with icy temperatures. Today, there are 120 wineries cultivating grapes in and around the Okanagan Valley. The main varietals include: Zweigelt, Gamy, Viognier and Pinot Gris, but also Merlot and Cabernet Sauvignon. In some places, such as the Naramatha Bench countryside north of Penticton, there is one winery after the other. Even the Osoyoos tribe in the south of the valley have moved with the times and are now also cultivating vines in their reserve.

Cherry harvest in the fertile Okanagan Valley, the fruit basket of Canada

a visit. On the eastern shore of the approximately 150km/93mi long Okanagan Lake is the main town of *Kelowna* (pop. 117,000), where the mild temperatures have attracted many retirees who spend their days playing golf and tennis.

## SIGHTSEEING

### GRAY MONK CELLARS 🌿

Learn all about Canadian wine here with hourly guided tours, followed by wine tasting, some spectacular views of the lake, and also a restaurant. *Daily in summer 10am–7pm, tours 11am–4pm, otherwise Mon–Sat 11am –5pm | admission free | Camp Rd. | Okanagan Centre*

### MISSION HILL WINERY ★ ●

A magnificent Tuscan-inspired estate high on the hill, surrounded by vineyards and orchards. The most important and attractive winery in the Okanagan Valley. *Daily in summer 9.30am–7pm, otherwise 10am–5pm | guide C$12 | 1730 Mission Hill Rd. | West Bank | www.missionhill winery.com*

### NK'MIP CELLARS ☺

The ultra modern winery and cultural centre of the Osoyoos Indians has impressive architecture that incorporates many sustainable Native American elements in its construction. The centre has a restaurant serving organic food, a large resort with golf course and a campground. *Daily in summer 9am–9pm, otherwise until 5pm | admission free, guided tours C$7.50 every 2 hours 11am–7pm | 1400 Rancher Creek Rd. | Osoyoos | www.nkmipcellars.com*

### O'KEEFE RANCH

Established in 1867, the cattle ranch was once the largest of British Columbia. Today, it is an open-air museum and its restored ranch house, post office, church and blacksmith provides some vivid insights into the life of the early pioneers. *Daily in summer 9am–6pm | admission C$12 | 9km/5.5mi north of Vernon on Hwy. 97*

## FOOD & DRINK

### EARL'S ON TOP RESTAURANT
Fish, steak and pasta on the shores of the lake, with terrace. *211 Bernard Ave. | Kelowna | tel. 250 7 63 27 77 | Moderate*

### INSIDER TIP ▶ QUAIL'S GATE ESTATE WINERY
Wine shop and terrace restaurant, very nice for lunch. *3303 Boucherie Rd. | West Bank | tel. 250 7 69 25 00 | www.quails gate.com | Budget–Moderate*

### SALTY'S BEACH HOUSE
Popular seafood restaurant on the lake beach. *1000 Lakeshore Dr. | Penticton | tel. 250 4 93 50 01 | Moderate*

## BEACHES

Beautiful beaches such as those in the ★ *Haynes Point Provincial Park* lie in the southern part of the valley at *Osoyoos* as well as in *Penticton* (large peach festival at the end of July).

## WHERE TO STAY

### ELDORADO ☆
Small, stylish hotel overlooking the lake. Restaurant on the veranda. *55 rooms | Pandosy St./Cook Rd. | Kelowna | tel. 250 7 63 75 00 | www.hotelelowna.com | Moderate–Expensive*

### RIVERSIDE MOTEL
Well-established, comfortable motel close to the shores of the lake, with swimming pool. *45 rooms | 110 Riverside Dr. | Penticton | tel. 250 4 92 26 15 | www. riversidemotel.ca | Budget–Moderate*

### SPARKLING HILL RESORT ● ☺
Super luxurious, environmentally friendly hotel that belongs to the Swarovski crystal family. The highlight: the 3.5 million crystals that were incorporated into the spectacular design. There is also the elegant and contemplative *KurSpa* with cold sauna and maple syrup treatments. *149 rooms | 888 Sparkling Place | Vernon | tel. 250 2 75 15 56 | www.sparklinghill.com | Expensive*

### WILDHORSE MOUNTAIN RANCH
B & B ranch in the calm of nature in an idyllic valley west of Okanagan Lake. Daily horse rides. *7 rooms | 25808 Wildhorse Rd. | Summerland | tel. 250 4 94 05 06 | www.wildhorsemountainranch.com | Budget–Moderate*

## INFORMATION

### THOMPSON OKANAGAN TOURISM
*544 Harvey Ave. | Kelowna | tel. 250 8 60 59 99 | www.totabc.org, www.tourism kelowna.com*

# QUEEN CHARLOTTE ISLANDS

**(132 A2–3) (⫫ B10–12) The often storm-tossed and rain-swept archipelago (pop. 6000) was once the realm of the warlike Haida Indians. They are now a kind of Galapagos of the north, with rainforests, sea lions, bald eagles, and an incredible variety of marine life.**

The northern *Graham Island* has an infra-structure of roads (ferry from Prince Rupert). A large part of the almost un-inhabited southern *Moresby Island* and its unique ecosystem is now part of the *Gwaii Haanas National Park*. The new *Haida Heritage Centre*, where the Haida have once again started to carve totem poles and canoes, is very interesting *(in* *summer, daily 9am– 6pm | admission C$15 | Skidegate).*

### BLUEWATER ADVENTURES
The company offers 5–11 day kayaking trips along the west coast, including the Queen Charlotte Islands. *3252 E First St. | North Vancouver | tel. 604 9 80 38 00 | www.bluewateradventures.ca*

### QUEEN CHARLOTTE ADVENTURES
Guided kayaking tours along the coast; also rental, ferry service, and boat transport if you want to do an independent trip. *Queen Charlotte City | tel. 250 5 59 89 90 | www.queencharlotteadventures.com*

## WHERE TO STAY

### GOLDEN SPRUCE
Simple motel, very centrally located on Graham Island; the helpful owner also organises trips and fishing expeditions. *Tel. 250 5 57 43 25 | www.goldenspruce. ca | Budget–Moderate*

# SUNSHINE COAST

**(133 D5) (*∅ D–E14*) The coast is protected by a series of small islands and is climate is very sunny and mild. It lies north of Vancouver and is perfect for a two to three day trip to explore its verdant fjord landscape.**

Hwy. 101 winds 140km/87mi along the coastal bays northwards until the road ends in *Lund*. Lining the way are marinas and sleepy fishing villages – today often home to artists and dropouts – and coastal parks such as the *Saltery Bay Provincial Park* (with campsites).

The unique and pristine ecosystem of Moresby Island

The fishing village of *Egmont* is the start of the impressive 4km/2.5mi long hike to the INSIDER TIP *Skookumchuck Narrows* – where the tide forces seawater through the narrows creating rapids and gigantic whirlpools.

## TOURS

### SUNSHINE COAST TOURS
Water taxi and tour service with boat trips to the Princess Louisa Inlet and to the Skookumchuck Narrows. They also have a service for diving and accommodation. *4289 Orca Rd. | Garden Bay | tel. 800 8 70 90 55 | www.sunshinecoasttours.bc.ca*

## WHERE TO STAY

### DESOLATION RESORT ✷ ☺

Resort on an isolated fjord with beautiful, ecologically designed wooden chalets right on the water. *12 rooms/apartments | Malaspina Rd. | Powell River | tel. 604 4 83 35 92 | www.desolationresort.com | Moderate–Expensive*

### HISTORIC LUND HOTEL & RV PARK

Heritage hotel that is owned and run by local Native Americans – renovated and right on the harbour. Camping, restaurant and tours organised. *31 rooms | Lund | tel. 604 4 14 04 74 | www.lundhotel.com | Budget–Moderate*

## LOW BUDGET

▶ A night in the most unusual hostel in Canada costs only C$21 (for members only C$17): the *Shuswap Lake Hostel (229 Trans-Canada Hwy. | Squilax/Chase | tel. 250 6 75 29 77 | www.hihostels.ca)* is in an old *general store*, and some of the rooms are renovated railway wagons. On request, the Greyhound bus stops right at the hostel.

▶ Even well known ski resorts like Whistler have some affordable restaurants, such as *Ingrid's Village Café (4305 Skier's Approach)*. The little coffee shop right in the pedestrianised zone is popular with the mountain bike and snow-board crowd and serves healthy, reasonably priced food. For C$7 you can tuck into a falafel burger with couscous.

### WEST COAST WILDERNESS LODGE ✷

Well-maintained country inn in a prime location on a cliff overlooking the fjord. *20 rooms | Egmont | tel. 604 8 83 36 67 | www.wcwl.com | Expensive*

# WELLS GRAY PROV. PARK

**(133 E–F3) (𝄜 F12–13) Stretching over 2000 square miles, the provincial park on the northern edge of the Columbia Mountains is an untamed forest wilderness known for its waterfalls.**

Among these are also the 137m/450ft high ★ *Helmcken Falls*, which plunges into a narrow valley. Just as spectacular is *Spahats Creek* that tumbles down a 120m/400ft deep gorge near the park entrance. Wilderness hikers can explore the reserve on the wide network of hiking trails and **INSIDER TIP** the *Clearwater* and *Azure Lake* chain of lakes are ideal for canoe trips. Accommodation and rental services are at the park entrance and in Clearwater. For information and help on planning even more isolated wilderness canoe trips, such as on *Hobson Lake*, contact *Lake Clearwater Lake Tours (Clearwater | tel. 250 6 74 21 21 | www.clearwaterlaketours.com)*.

# WHISTLER

**(133 D–E5) (𝄜 E14) The well-maintained winter sports resort (pop. 10,000), about two hour's drive north of Vancouver, was the venue for the alpine events of the 2010 Winter Olympics.**

It is hard to believe that the small town in the snowy *Coast Mountains* was only laid out 50 years ago. However, with two mountains, *Whistler* and *Blackcomb*

*Mountain*, and nearly 40 ski lifts it is a superlative ski resort. Some of the lifts also operate in the summer, making it easy to walk, bike or go glacier skiing in the summit region. Below in the valley life plays out around the pedestrian zone of *Whistler Village* lined with shops, restaurants and cafés.

The journey to Whistler is in itself worthwhile, the ❄ *Sea to Sky Highway* (Hwy. 99), with fabulous views across Howe Sound, curves the along the banks of the mine. *Daily 9am–5.30pm | admission (guided tour) C$21.50 | on Hwy. 99 at Britannia Beach*

## FOOD & DRINK

### BEARFOOT BISTRO
Serving fine west coast cuisine: caribou tartar with shallot and thyme puree, salmon in herb crab butter – and wonderful desserts. *4121 Village Green | tel. 604 9 32 34 33 | Moderate–Expensive*

2010 Winter Olympics were held in the snowy mountains around Whistler

deep fjords with several viewing points, numerous spectacular waterfalls and info boards that outlines the history of the Native Americans in the region.

## SIGHTSEEING

### BC MUSEUM OF MINING
Old tunnels, jackhammers, panning for gold, and a giant truck are the attractions of this mining museum in an old copper

### BRASSERIE DES ARTISTES
Popular terrace in the pedestrian area, ideal to sit and people watch. Breakfast also good. *4232 Village Stroll | tel. 604 9 32 35 69 | Budget*

### STEEP'S GRILL ❄
Restaurant with wonderful views of the Coast Mountains. *At the Whistler Mountain gondola station | tel. 604 9 05 23 79 | Moderate*

## WHERE TO STAY

### EDGEWATER LODGE

Somewhat outside of town, but with its own lake shore and a restaurant that serves excellent wild game dishes. *12 rooms | 8841 Hwy. 99 | tel. 604 9 32 06 88 | www.edgewaterlodge.com | Moderate*

### FAIRMONT CHATEAU WHISTLER

Luxurious and elegant, the hotel is perfectly situated close to the valley ski lifts. Good golf course. *550 rooms | Whistler Village | tel. 604 9 38 80 00 | www.fairmont.com | Expensive*

### MOUNTAINSIDE LODGE

A modern time share facility close to the pedestrian area and the ski lifts. Often cheap deals. *4417 Sundial Place | tel. 604 9 32 45 11 | www.shellhospitality.com | Budget–Moderate*

## INFORMATION

### TOURISM WHISTLER

Information centre: *4230 Gateway Dr. | tel. 604 9 35 33 57 | www.whistler.com*

# YELLOWHEAD REGION

*(132–133 B–F 1–3) (Ø C–E 10–11)*
**Yellowhead Highway 16 opened in 1970 and is the second major east-west highway in western Canada, apart from the Trans-Canada Highway further south.**

From the prairies, it runs via Edmonton and Jasper through the isolated north to the Pacific. It follows the old pack route of the fur traders and provides access to the far north of British Columbia (by means of secondary roads such as the Cassiar Highway). The road is named after a blond fur trader whose image is still shown today on the road signs.

## SIGHTSEEING

### FORT ST. JAMES ★ ●
**(133 D2) (Ø E11)**

The fur trading post, founded by Simon Fraser in 1806, has been restored to an excellent museum village that really brings to life the era of the fur traders, in summer you can even spend the night in the historic *Officer's House (tel. 250 9 96 71 91 | www.pc.gc.ca/stjames | Moderate incl. catering). Daily in summer 9am–5pm | admission C$8 | 50k/30mi north of Vanderhoof on Hwy. 27*

### 'KSAN INDIAN VILLAGE
**(132 C1) (Ø D10)**

An open-air museum village of the Git'ksan tribe, with totem poles and carvings. Dance performances in the summer. *Daily in summer 9am–5pm | admission C$2 | guide C$10 | Hazelton*

### TOWNS ALONG YELLOWHEAD HIGHWAY

From the border to Alberta, in Jasper National Park, the highway first crosses the dense forests of the Fraser Plateau. West of the logging town (pop. 72,000) of *Prince George* **(133 D2) (Ø E11))** the route then passes through a massive lake district to the Coast Mountains, where the realm of the Northwest Coast Indians begins. At *Moricetown Canyon* on the Bulkley River you can watch them fishing salmon in the traditional way during July and August. Nearby, in the *Hazelton* **(132 C1) (Ø D10)** area are the reserve villages of the Tsimshian Indians, with ancient totem poles that attest to the wood craft skills of the tribe. Accommodation tip: *Smithers Guest House (5 rooms | 1766 Main St. | Smithers | tel. 250 8 47*

When the salmon run grizzly bears have rich pickings in the waters of British Columbia

*48 62 | Budget)*, a comfortable B & B within walking distance from the centre of town. *Prince Rupert* (pop. 15,000) **(132 B2)** *(𝄞 C11)* an important fishing, coal and grain port at the western end of *Yellowhead Highway*, provides access to the ferry system along the west coast: the *BC Ferries* run from here south to Vancouver Island, the ships of *Alaska Marine Highway* northwards to Alaska.

## TOURS

### PRINCE RUPERT ADVENTURE TOURS

The company organises half day boat excursions to watch grizzly bears in the Khuzemateen reservation area. *207 3rd Ave. E | Prince Rupert | tel. 250 6 27 91 66 | www.adventuretours.net*

## INFORMATION

### PRINCE GEORGE VISITOR CENTRE

*1300 First Ave., Suite 101 | Prince George | tel. 250 5 62 37 00 | www.tourismpg.com, www.hellobc.com/nbc*

## WHERE TO GO

### STEWART

**(132 B1)** *(𝄞 C10)*

From Kitwanga the *Cassiar Highway* provides a detour into the mountainous region on the border to Alaska. It is 240km/150mi to the town of Stewart at the end of a 145km/90mi long fjord and the pleasantly run down neighbouring town of *Hyder* is where Alaska begins – easily identifiable because the bars do not have a curfew. In *Fish Creek* on the outskirts of Hyder, the silver salmon spawn in the summer and you can often see bears and bald eagles, as they gorge on the fish. The ☀ dirt road along the Fish Creek leads a good 30km/18mi further up into the mountains with some splendid views of Salmon Glacier. Comfortable accommodation with a Wild West feel at the INSIDER TIP *Ripley Creek Inn (32 rooms | Stewart | tel. 250 6 36 23 44 | Budget–Moderate*. Their rooms are situated in several lovingly restored historic houses and cabins; the inn also has a good restaurant.

# ROCKY MOUNTAINS

**Whether on postcards or in coffee table books, you will have seen the pictures: emerald glacial lakes, rugged peaks, colourful wild flower meadows and grizzlies picking blueberries.**

The Rockies region offers all the clichés commonly associated with Canada. So it is not surprising then that the mountains on the border between Alberta and British Columbia are also the most famous and most popular tourist region in western Canada. Five major national parks attract visitors, four of them – Banff, Jasper, Kootenay and Yoho – border on each other and form a nature reserve area that covers 7700 square miles. Magnificent

mountains at their best – accessible yet unsullied by alpine huts and highways. To date only four passes lead through the Canadian Rockies and only a few highways (albeit spectacular ones) access the region. However, the parks have a very good network of hiking trails. In midsummer, there is a massive influx of visitors to the more well known areas such as Banff, Jasper and Lake Louise. Hotels are usually fully booked, and if you do not have a reservation, it will be difficult to find a place to rest your head. You will have better luck at the campsites and at the edge of the parks in places such as Canmore. The Rockies are the easternmost

Photo: Maligne Canyon in Jasper National Park

The most spectacular road in the world: the Rockies have a network of some of the most scenic national parks in Canada

section of the North American Cordillera and Canada, the mighty Rocky Mountains stretch 1200km/745mi before ending in the Yukon. The mountain range consists of sedimentary rocks, shale, limestone and sandstone, which lay in deposits in a primordial seabed. 60 million years ago the mountains were formed by tectonic forces, glaciers then carved out valleys, leaving behind lakes and large moraines –

a stunning backdrop for nature lovers and wilderness enthusiasts.

# BANFF NAT. PARK

(134 C4–5) (*ᗕ H13*) The oldest national park in Canada is 2564 square miles of

Lake Louise: a crystal clear mountain lake, a magnificent castle hotel and towering peaks

**glacier valleys, emerald lakes, dense forests and snow–capped mountains in the Bow River valley.**

In 1885, when the railway was arrived in this region, the Canadian government decided to make the mountain landscape a nature reserve. Due to the strict regulations only a small part of the park was opened to the public, including the town *Banff* (pop. 5000) and some ski areas. On the summit of the *Sulphur Mountain* a ゞゝ gondola leads to a vantage point overlooking the city and the Bow River. Some hotels were built along *Lake Louise*, but around these oases of civilisation the mountain wilderness stretches, as it has since time immemorial. Park wardens in the Banff or Lake Louise visitor centres have hiking maps for more than 1300km/810mi of trails in the hinterland.

## SIGHTSEEING

### BANFF PARK MUSEUM
A log cabin dating from 1903 houses the oldest natural history museum in western Canada, on the banks of the Bow River. *Daily in the summer 10am–6pm, otherwise 1pm–5pm | admission C$4. 91 | Banff Ave. | Banff*

### CAVE AND BASIN
### NATIONAL HISTORIC SITE
Newly designed exhibitions about the park's history, housed in the old bath house of the hot springs – the reason for the park's origin – and all around you will find beautiful nature trails, including the *Marsh Trail (Cave Ave. | Banff)* with its many lookout points.

### FAIRMONT BANFF SPRINGS HOTEL ゞゝ
The ostentatious hotel rises out of the forest at the end of Spray Avenue in Banff; it was built in 1886 by the Canadian Pacific Railroad. The railway director William Cornelius Van Horne was the driving force behind the construction of this majestic castle hotel. His belief was, 'If we cannot export the scenery, we must import the tourists' so along with the Trans-Canadian Railway (completed in 1885) he also had a series of luxury hotels constructed. The Banff Springs is one of the most beautiful examples of these 'railway hotels'.

### ICEFIELDS PARKWAY ★

'The most spectacular journey in the world' is the byline of the 230km/143mi Highway 93 from Lake Louise to Jasper. The road runs along the ridge of the mountains past ancient glaciers and alpine lakes, waterfalls and sweeping summits. It is pays to start the journey early, all the best views are to the west, and the morning sun catches the rock walls and ice falls in a soft glow. And keep your camera ready, because quite often you will catch the park's animals along the way: a Wapiti deer or moose, mountain sheep or goats – and with a little luck even a grizzly. Especially in May and June the bears and mountain sheep can be seen in the snow-free valleys.

The most beautiful views, await at ● ⬇ *Bow Summit Pass* viewpoint (2000m/ 6560ft) with the remarkable milky-green of *Peyto Lake* and the canyons further up the valley. Other worthwhile stops include: *Mistaya Canyon*, *Waterfowl Lake* with a beautiful campground and the *Sunwapta Falls*.

### LAKE LOUISE ★

Canada's most famous lake shimmers in turquoise at the foot of the 3464m/ 11,365ft Mount Victoria. On the waterfront at *Chateau Lake Louise* (another railway hotel) there is a constant hustle and bustle, but on the paths around it are much quieter. Nice for a day hike are trails such as *Big Beehive/Lake AgnesTtrail* or the *Plain of Six Glaciers Trail*. Another picture-perfect lake is 15km/9mi further south, ⬇ *Moraine Lake* in the *Valley of Ten Peaks*.

### WHYTE MUSEUM OF THE ROCKIES

Exhibitions about the Rocky Mountains, the pioneer era and the first Swiss mountain guide. Guided tours to two pioneer cabins. *Daily 10am–5pm | admission C$8 | 111 Bear St. | Banff*

## FOOD & DRINK

### COYOTE'S ⊙

Pleasant bistro with creative southwestern cuisine. Also gluten-free dishes and

---

**MARCO POLO HIGHLIGHTS**

organic ingredients. Breakfast, lunch and dinner. *206 Caribou St. Banff | tel. 403 7 62 39 63 | Moderate*

### JUNIPER BISTRO ☆☆ ☺

Fine organic cuisine with many regional ingredients and magnificent views over Banff. In the newly renovated *Juniper Hotel (Moderate–Expensive. 1 Juniper Way | Banff | tel. 403 7 62 22 81 | Moderate–Expensive*

### LAKE LOUISE STATION RESTAURANT

Refined regional cuisine in an old Canadian Pacific railway station. A classic and unique dining experience. *Lake Louise | tel. 403 5 22 26 00 | www.lakelouisestation.com | Moderate–Expensive*

### INSIDER TIP NUM-TI-JAH LODGE

Good place for a break on your drive on the Icefields Parkway: a historic lodge on the shore of Bow Lake. Traditional furnishings and a good restaurant. *Icefields Parkway | 40km/25mi north of Lake Louise | tel. 403 5 22 21 67 | www.sntj.ca | Budget–Moderate*

### SALTLIK

Chic restaurant with a large bar on the ground floor. Serves steaks and fresh fish daily. *221 Bear St. | Banff | tel. 403 7 62 24 67 | Moderate–Expensive*

### SUSHI HOUSE

Tiny but excellent, the sushi comes to the table by model train. *304 Caribou St. | Banff | tel. 403 7 62 43 53 | Budget*

### WILD BILL'S LEGENDARY SALOON

Hearty Wild West food, lots of wooden decor and plenty of beer make for an excellent atmosphere. ☆☆ Nice balcony with a view over the action in Banff Avenue. *201 Banff Ave. | Banff | tel. 403 7 62 03 33 | Budget–Moderate*

## SHOPPING

Banff Avenue is full of souvenir shops selling t-shirts, fleeces and chocolates temptations. You will find better quality and choice, in the shops in the side streets such as in INSIDER TIP *Canada House Gallery (201 Bear St.),* selling arts and crafts only produced in Canada.

## SPORTS & ACTIVITIES

### ADVENTURES UNLIMITED

Here you can arrange all kinds of active tours in the national parks: horseback riding, guided hiking tours, rafting trips and in winter even dog sledding. *211 Bear St. | Banff | tel. 403 7 62 45 54 | www.banff adventures.com*

### BACTRAX BIKE RENTAL

Bike rental for day trips in and around Banff. Good tips for routes. *225 Bear St. | tel. 403 7 62 81 77 | www.snowtips-bactrax. com*

### ICEFIELD HELICOPTER TOURS

Spectacular helicopter excursions over the Central Rockies and the Columbia Icefield. Starts on Hwy. 11 40km/25mi east of the Icefields Parkway. *Cline River | Hwy. 11 | tel. 1888 8 44 35 14 403 7 21 21 00 | www.icefieldheli.com*

### UPPER HOT SPRINGS

Relax those muscles after your hike in a steaming bath. *Daily in the summer 9am–11pm, otherwise 10am–10pm | admission C$7.50 | Mountain Ave. | Banff | www.hot springs.ca*

### HIKES

Just on the outskirts of Banff there are already some shorter hikes, such as the *Fenland Trail* (just under a mile), into the *Vermillion Lakes* area. Despite its proxim-

Western Canada's famous resort Banff is located in a beautiful mountain setting

ity to the Trans-Canada Highway, Wapiti deer, moose, and beaver are often spotted on the trail. From the parking lot of the Mount Norquay ski area a 2km/1.2mi long hiking trail leads up to the summit of the ☆ *Stoney Squaw Mountain* and a breathtaking panoramic view over the Banff Valley and *Lake Minnewanka*. Other good hiking destinations for day trips are the valley of the Spray River, the *Sunshine Meadows* and the *Johnstone Canyon*. Also highly recommended are the trails that begin at Lake Louise and nearby Moraine Lake, over the *Sentinel Pass* in the *Paradise Valley* or to the *Wenkchemna Pass*.

## WHERE TO STAY

In the height of summer it is best to book several months in advance for accommodation.

### INSIDER TIP ▶ BAKER CREEK CHALETS

Canadian idyll – with well-maintained log cabins and a bubbling brook – in the middle of the park, 15 minutes drive from Lake Louise. *33 rooms | Hwy. 1A | Lake Louise | tel. 403 5 22 37 61 | www.baker creek.com | Expensive*

### BANFF CARIBOU LODGE

Mid to upper range modern hotel. Pleasant, centrally located in the town. *185 rooms | 521 Banff Ave. | Banff | tel. 403 7 62 58 87 | www.bestofbanff.com | Moderate–Expensive*

### DEER LODGE

Small, historic and elegant hotel just a few minutes' walk from Lake Louise. *71 rooms | Lake Louise | tel. 403 5 22 39 91 | www.crmr.com | Moderate–Expensive*

### ELKHORN LODGE

Simple little motel, well situated in a quiet location close to Banff Avenue. *9 rooms | 124 Spray Ave. | Banff | tel. 403 7 62 22 99 | www.elkhornbanff.ca | Budget–Moderate*

### ODENTHAL'S B & B

A simple B & B in a heritage home, with lots of personal attention from the gracious hosts. *2 rooms | 510 Buffalo St. | tel. 403 7 62 20 81 | Budget*

### Y MOUNTAIN LODGE

Alternative hostel located in Banff, on the banks of the Bow River. Very cheap 6 and 10 bed dorm rooms and 42 double rooms; kitchen and laundry. *102 Spray Ave. | Banff | tel. 403 7 62 35 60 | www.ymountainlodge. com | Moderate–Expensive*

River valley is ideal for multi-day hiking trips. Various shorter trails lead from Highway 93 (which goes through the park) such as one along the *Marble Canyon* and one to the bright orange and ochre *Paint Pots* where Native Americans harvested their colours for war paint.

When your muscles are sore from hiking you can relax at the southern entrance to the park where hot water bubbles ups

Enjoy a relaxing soak in the hot springs of the Kootenay National Park

### BANFF NATIONAL PARK

Visitor centre on Highway 1 in Lake Louise and Banff. *224 Banff Ave. | tel. 403 7 62 15 50 | www.parkscanada.ca, www.banff lakelouise.com*

### KOOTENAY NATIONAL PARK
(134 C5) (*Ω H14*)

The largely unspoilt 543 square miles nature reserve area around the Kootenay

(sometimes at hot as 47°C/116°F) at the ● *Radium Hot Springs (admission C$6.40 | www.hotsprings.ca)* the largest (25m/82ft) mineral bathing pools in Canada. A good tip for nature lovers is at the southern edge of the park in the valley of the Kootenay River. The ☺ INSIDER TIP *Cross River Wilderness Centre (Settlers Rd. | Radium Hot Springs | tel. 403 2 71 32 96 | www.canadianrockies.net/crossriver | Moderate)* has eight cabins and tepees that are solar powered, and all around you will find wonderful hiking areas of far from civilisation.

# CROWSNEST PASS

(134–135 C–D6) *(ω H14)* **The Crowsnest Pass is the southernmost pass over the Canadian Rockies.**

The pass was once an important Native American trade route, today the modern Highway 3 crosses through the densely forested mountains at a height of 1396m/ 4580ft. Crowsnest Pass has a series of small towns, such as *Bellevue*, *Frank* and *Coleman,* located along the highway. They were all established around 1900 as mining towns. Frank is infamous for a massive landslide in 1903 that buried the village and killed 60 people. An excellent museum, the *Frank Slide Interpretive Centre (daily in the summer 9am–6pm, otherwise 5pm | admission C$10)* shows the pioneer history of the region, the avalanche and also a trail that winds through the rocks of *Frank Slide.*

The *Tecumseh Mountain Ranch (6 cabins | Hwy. 3 Crowsnest Pass | Blairmore | tel. 403 5 63 39 00 | www.mountainguestranch. com | Budget–Moderate)* is a rustic ranch in very pleasant surroundings, just behind the border to Alberta. Accommodation is in log cabins and campsites.

# JASPER NAT. PARK

(134 B–C 3–4) *(ω G 12–13)* **The gleaming white Athabasca Glacier, whose edge is close to the Icefields Parkway, is a highlight of the Rockies.**

The *Parker Ridge Trail* is a short hike that offers more views of the glacier. The 4170 square mile park offers even more: the roaring *Athabasca Falls* on the Icefields

Parkway and the idyllic ✳️ *Maligne Lake* or a relaxing soak in the hot springs of *Miette.* Accommodation and restaurants can be found in the only village within in the park, *Jasper.*

## SIGHTSEEING

### ATHABASCA GLACIER

The glacier is part of the 126 square mile *Columbia Icefield,* a remnant from the last ice age, which sends its melt water into three oceans, the Atlantic, Pacific, and Arctic. As recently as 100 years ago ice

## LOW BUDGET

▶ Admission to Banff National Park costs just C$9.80. For a larger round trip the *National Passport* is the cheaper option: C$67.70 per person, C$136.40 for up to seven people in a car – valid for a year for all nine national parks in Alberta and British Columbia.

▶ Youth hostels are rather rare in Canada, but there are about a dozen in prime locations in the Rockies. Some luxurious, some rustic, but all ideal for a bike ride, for instance on the Icefields Parkway. From C$18 to C$24 (for non–members) no age restriction, *www.hihostels.ca*

▶ *Bruno's Bar & Grill (304 Caribou Street)* in Banff serves breakfast until late in the afternoon, also good burgers and chunky sandwiches – almost all for under C$10. There is also live music in the evenings.

Icy water sports: glacial Maligne Lake in Jasper National Park

filled the entire valley where Hwy. 93 is today. Signs on the roadside indicate just how fast the glacier is retreating. The tours offered to the glacier in specially adapted vehicles are more of a tourist trap. However, you can also go on your own or take a guided hike with *Ice Walk* (info: visitor centre on Hwy. 93). South of the Athabasca Glacier is the ✴ *Glacier Skywalk* (due to open in May 2014) a glass-floored platform stretching out over the *Sunwapta Valley* – with great views and plenty of thrills.

### JASPER TRAMWAY

Gondola on the ✴ *Whistler Mountain* offering magnificent panoramic views over the valley of Jasper. There are walking paths around the summit. *Daily in the summer 9am–8pm, otherwise 10am–5pm | ticket C$31 | Whistler Rd. | Jasper*

### MALIGNE CANYON

Six bridges, steep stairs and an interpretive hiking trail provide access to a spec-

tacular sheer drop gorge on the Maligne River which makes its thunderous way through the rocks. With restaurant. *Maligne Lake Rd., approx. 20km/12.5mi east of Jasper*

## TOURS

### MALIGNE LAKE BOAT TOURS

One and a half hour cruises on the largest glacier lake in the Rockies on the famous *Spirit Island.* The best time is in the afternoon. *In the summer daily on the hour 10am–5pm | ticket C$55, reservation in Jasper | 616 Patricia St. | tel. 780 8 52 33 70*

### SKYLINE TRAIL RIDES

Half-day horse rides, but also three-day trail rides with overnight stay in a wilderness lodge. Reserve in advance. *Tel. 780 8 52 42 15 | www.skylinetrail.com*

### HIKES

Find the most beautiful and most popular trails for short hikes are at the foot of

*Mount Edith Cavell* and at *Maligne Canyon.* Especially suitable for day hikes and longer trips are the *Tonquin Valley* and the wilderness region to the *Brazeau Lake.*

## FOOD & DRINK

### PAPA GEORGE'S
Cosy bar in the Astoria Hotel serving steaks and fish dishes. *404 Connaught Dr. | Jasper | tel. 780 8 52 33 51 | Moderate*

### SOMETHING ELSE RESTAURANT
Serving Greek food such as souvlaki and moussaka, but also pizzas and steaks. *621 Patricia St. | Jasper | tel. 780 8 52 38 50 | Budget–Moderate*

## WHERE TO STAY

### ALPINE VILLAGE
Neat log cabins in the Athabasca River Valley. Pleasantly furnished, with an open fireplace. *41 rooms | Hwy. 93A East | Jasper | tel. 780 8 52 32 85 | www.alpinevillage jasper.com | Moderate–Expensive*

### FAIRMONT JASPER PARK LODGE ★
This is the luxury version of a log cabin in the wilderness: the sophisticated resort hotel is located in a large park on the outskirts of Jasper and overlooks its own private lake. There are rooms in the main building and attractive old log cabins with fireplace. Somewhat busy in high season, otherwise very comfortable and peaceful, also an 18 hole golf course and four tennis courts. *746 rooms | Jasper | tel. 780 8 52 33 01 | www.fairmont.com | Expensive*

### INSIDER TIP TEKARRA LODGE
Rustic log cabins with fireplace, on the outskirts of Jasper. Beautiful riverside location and good restaurant. *42 rooms | Hwy. 93A S | tel. 780 8 52 30 58 | www.tekarralodge.com | Moderate–Expensive*

## INFORMATION

### JASPER NATIONAL PARK
Information centre opposite the train station on the main road. *Jasper | tel. 780 8 52 62 36 | www.jasper.travel*

## WHERE TO GO

### MOUNT ROBSON PROV. PARK
(134 B3–4) *(∅ G12)*
To the west of Jasper is the highest peak in the Rockies, the 3954m/12,973ft summit of Mount Robson. In good weather the mountain is visible from the Highway 16. Recommended: one to two day hike along the Robson River at the foot of the ice-covered massif. A pleasant overnight option with views of the mountain is ☆ *Mountain River Lodge (4 rooms | Hwy. 16 | Valemount | tel. 250 5 66 98 99 | www.mtrobson.com | Budget–Moderate).*

# KANANASKIS COUNTRY

(134–135 C–D5) *(∅ H14)* ★ ● **Banff may be more famous, however, this recreation area between Banff and Calgary, on the sunny eastern edge of the Rockies, is just as attractive – and there are no entrance fees.**

The majority of the Kananaskis Valley is a nature reserve and offers excellent sports activities including a championship golf course and a vast network of hiking and cycling paths. The *Peter Lougheed Provincial Park* at the southern end of the valley is particularly popular with its lakes framed by 3000m/9850ft peaks. There are some good hiking on the trails around the *Highwood Pass,* on the trail to *Ribbon Falls* and the ☆ INSIDER TIP *Mount Indefatigable Trail* with lovely views.

## WHERE TO STAY

### DELTA LODGE AT KANANASKIS
Modern, quiet facility in the heart of the region, a good base for golfers and hikers. *412 rooms | Kananaskis Village | tel. 403 5 91 77 11 | www.deltahotels.com | Moderate–Expensive*

A Bavarian water hydrant in Kimberley

### INSIDER TIP ▶ MT. ENGADINE LODGE
Secluded in a high valley this rustic mountain inn is perfectly situated for hikers. Also open in winter. *5 rooms and 2 cabins | Canmore | tel. 403 6 78 40 80 | www.mountengadine.com | incl. full board Moderate*

## WHERE TO GO

### COWBOY TRAIL ☆ (135 D5) (*𝕄 H14*)
An hour's drive east of Kananaskis on Hwy. 22, the Cowboy Trail is a panoramic drive that runs through the ranch country at the foothills of the Rockies. Worth seeing is the *Bar U Ranch*, near *Longview*, a National Historic Site and original 1882 ranch that preserves Alberta's cowboy history. Also horse-drawn carriage rides and exhibitions.

# KIMBERLEY

*(134 C6) (𝕄 H14)* **This town (pop. 6600) on the western edge of the Rocky Mountains is known as the 'Bavarian City of the Rockies'.**
When the local mine closed in 1972 and it seemed that the town would become a ghost town, the city fathers decided to turn their town into a Bavarian village. The mountain scenery is the ideal backdrop and the architecture is now thoroughly alpine. The shops on The Platzl pedestrian zone sell Bavarian knickknacks; there is an outsize cuckoo clock and in the restaurants the bands play traditional German music. Even the fire hydrants wear painted *lederhosen* and *dirndl*.
The INSIDER TIP ▶ *Hillside Garden View (440 Spokane St. | tel. 250 4 27 46 81 | Moderate)* serves tasty sandwiches and homemade soup in a garden that has a miniature Swiss village and carvings. At *Kootenay Rockies Tourism (1905 Warren Ave. | tel. 250 4 27 48 38 | www.kootenayrockies.com)* there is information about accommodation, ranches, golf courses and hiking trails in the region.

## WHERE TO GO

### FORT STEELE ★ (134 C6) (*𝕄 H14*)
About 30km/18mi east in the valley of the Columbia River the young gold rush era is brought to life in the Fort Steele heritage town. It was founded in 1865 as a post for the North West Mounted Police and soon became the largest settlement in the

region – although it was soon forgotten after the gold rush. Today it lives on as a museum town and more than 60 buildings have been restored or moved here from the surrounding area, costumed actors enact the life of the pioneers, there are heritage livestock displays and a stage-coach *(performances July/August daily 9.30am–6.30pm | admission C$7).* Accommodation is in an old Indian Residential school and mission run by Native Americans, the *St. Eugene Resort (125 rooms | 7777 Mission Rd. | Cranbrook | tel. 250 4 20 20 00 | www.steugene.ca | Moderate)* with good golf course and casino.

# WATERTON LAKES NAT. PARK

(135 D6) *(ꕤ H14–15)* **The 203 square mile park on the edge of the prairies was named after the series of lakes that stretch over the border to the Glacier National Park in Montana, USA.**

Good hiking trails lead into the hinterland which is still completely pristine. A particularly beautiful short hiking trail is the trail to the *Red Rock Canyon,* whose fiery red walls are made up of 1.5 billion year old sediment stone.

At *Cameron Lake* you can hire boats and canoes, and at the northern edge of the park you can observe a small herd of bison in an enclosure. The best views of the lake and mountains is to be had from the 🍂 terrace of the *Prince of Wales Hotel* at the northern edge of *Waterton Park,* the only village in the reserve.

## TOURS

**WATERTON SHORELINE CRUISES ★ ●**
The company offers boat trips on the 🍂 *Upper Waterton Lake.* The southernmost point of the cruise is in the *Glacier National Park* in Montana, USA. The views of the majestic mountains are especially good in the early morning. There is also a ferry

During the gold rush a thriving village: the museum village of Fort Steele

Emerald Lake in Yoho National Park lives up to its name

service for hikers. *Departure from the Waterton marina summer daily 10am, 1pm, 4pm, 7pm | ticket C$40 | tel. 403 8 59 23 62 | www.watertoncruise.com*

### CRYPT LAKE HIKE
The INSIDER TIP most unusual day hike in the Canadian Rockies, costs only C$20 or the price of the ferry ride over Waterton Lake. From the other shore the trail runs steeply uphill and finally via a ladder and through a tunnel to *Crypt Lake* high in the mountains of the park. *Daily departures summer 9am and 10am | Waterton Townsite*

## WHERE TO STAY

### NORTHLANDS LODGE
Stylishly renovated rustic country lodge, built in 1929, in the small town of Waterton Lakes. *9 rooms | 408 Evergreen Ave. | Waterton Park | tel. 403 8 59 23 53 |* www.northlandlodgecanada.com | *Moderate*

### WATERTON LAKES LODGE
Tastefully furnished rooms, some have a fireplace and there is also an adjacent youth hostel. *80 rooms | 101 Clematis Ave. | Waterton Park | tel. 403 8 59 21 50 | www.watertonlakeslodge.com | Moderate– Expensive*

# YOHO NAT. PARK

**(134 B–C4) *(ɷ G13)* The park in the valleys of the Kicking Horse and Yoho rivers on the western flank of the Rocky Mountains National Park is 'only' 507 square miles and not anywhere near as well known as its neighbouring big brother, the Banff National Park.**

This makes it far quieter but no less spectacular, with stunning nature and beautiful mountain scenery including the second highest waterfalls in Canada. You can explore Yoho National Park in a day trip from Lake Louise or Banff.

## SIGHTSEEING

### EMERALD LAKE ☀

The shimmering turquoise lake, surrounded by towering mountain peaks is very impressive and there are also some very scenic hiking trails on the glacier mountain slopes. A canoe (rentals at the lake) trip is especially beautiful in the summer.

### KICKING HORSE PASS

The Trans-Canada Highway traverses the national Park and climbs up to the Kicking Horse Pass (1647m/5403ft) over the watershed between Pacific and Arctic Ocean. To cope with the large differences in height, the railway engineers drilled two spiral tunnels into the mountain here 100 years ago. A curious sight is when you see freight trains with more than 100 wagons exiting the upper part of the tunnel while the last wagons are still entering.

### TAKAKKAW FALLS ★

A magnificent spectacle of nature is provided by the 344m/1130ft high Takakkaw Falls which is fed by melt water from the *Wapta Icefield*. The falls are the second highest in Canada, and are around 5km/3mi north of the icefield. `INSIDER TIP` In the afternoons the water cascades forcefully into the depths when the noonday sun melts the glacial ice.

## WHERE TO STAY

### EMERALD LAKE LODGE

Neat, quiet hotel with a good restaurant. Accommodation is in large log cabins on the lake. *85 rooms | Field | tel. 250 3 43 63 21 | www.crmr.com | Expensive*

### `INSIDER TIP` KICKING HORSE LODGE

Modern small lodge centrally situated but near the railway line. There is also an excellent ☺ restaurant next door, which serves regional organic cuisine. *14 rooms | Field | 100 Centre St. | tel. 250 3 43 63 03 | www.trufflepigs.com | Moderate*

## INFORMATION & TOURS

### YOHO VISITOR CENTRE

Visitor centre with a small museum. There are guided walks several times a week to the fossils of *Burgess Shale,* slate rocks from the Cambrian period. *Hwy. 1 | Field | tel. 250 3 43 67 83 | www.burgess-shale. bc.ca*

# FUR TRAPPER FOOD?

In a nature loving and wildlife-rich country such as Canada one would expect to see more tasty wild duck or juicy moose steak on the menu. Far from it! By law all privately shot game may be consumed privately – wild game for restaurants, however, must come from a farm. So Canadians hunt exclusively for personal consumption and at best you can enjoy wild game by private invitation, but the hunting season is in autumn and by the time the next visitors arrive in the spring the bear steaks will have long since been eaten.

# ALBERTA

The glacier-covered Rocky Mountains are the most spectacular and famous region of the province of Alberta. But one should also not forget the vast remainder of this area as the Rockies only make up a small part – along the extreme western border – of the 255,200 square mile province.

East of the mountains the endless prairies of central Canada stretch out into the vast subarctic forest area of the north. Despite the Rockies tourism, Alberta is above all a land of farmers and ranchers interspersed with small, sleepy villages. However, cowboy and trapper nostalgia does not reign throughout the province. Alberta is also a land of oil workers and high-tech energy companies. In 1914, the first oil well gushed in Turner Valley near Calgary; in 1947 further large oil deposits were discovered near the provincial capital Edmonton. Since then, the two cities – fierce rivals – have boomed, and the oil-rich province provides close to 80 per cent of Canada's fossil energy resources. The Mesozoic era left the province not only oil and coal: at that time dinosaurs lived in large swamps on the edge of a prehistoric lake and their fossilized bones appear everywhere in the sediment layers of river banks and gullies in southern Alberta. Alberta is the largest dinosaur graveyard in the world – much to the delight of all dinosaur fans.

Land of wheat and forests: buried beneath the wide prairies of Alberta there are both oil treasures and dinosaurs

**WHERE TO START?**
An easy to find starting point is the **Calgary Tower** on 101 9th Ave. Opposite the tower is the Glenbow Museum. The Stephen Avenue Mall is to the north, and the Eau Claire Market on the banks of the Bow River is another seven streets north.

# CALGARY

(135 D5) *(∅ H J 13–14)* **Skyscrapers, boutiques, sidewalk cafés and urban sculptures – Calgary (pop. 1.2 million) is a thriving metropolis.**

Stroll through the Stephen Avenue Mall, at the eastern end are the green lawns of the ● *Olympic Plaza* (often free concerts

In boomtown Calgary everything seems much larger – be it sculptures or buildings

in the summer) and you will get the feeling that the city is a proud Manhattan of the prairie. There is reason enough for all the excess and ostentatious cars: the oil boom in recent years has brought rapid growth to the city of the 1988 Winter Olympics. Calgary's history began in 1875 with the establishment of a police post along the Bow River to combat the trade in illegal whiskey. In 1883 the arrival of the Trans-Canada railway line in the prairies meant that soon after the first ranches were established and Calgary became the centre of the Canadian meat industry. The oil fund in Turner Valley (1914) triggered the first oil boom in Canada – and then it Calgary took off. However, the city still likes to maintain its cowboy image and for the past century has hosted the largest rodeo in the world in July, the *Calgary Stampede*.

## SIGHTSEEING

### CALGARY TOWER ⚜
On a clear day the panoramic view from this 191m/630ft tower (with revolving restaurant) is incredible. *Daily in summer*

*9am–10pm, otherwise until 9pm | admission C$15.50 | 9th Ave. | Centre St.*

### CANADA OLYMPIC PARK
The old Olympic centre's *Sports Hall of Fame (Tue–Sat 10am–5pm, Sun noon–5pm | admission C$12)* has everything you want to know about sport in Canada. There is also a zip line over the ski jump, mountain biking trails and bobsleigh rides in the summer. *Activities from end June–beginning Oct | ticket C$24– C$99 | on the western edge of the city, Hwy. 1*

### GLENBOW MUSEUM
The history of the Native Americans and settlers in western Canada is documented in three floors of exhibits. *Daily 9am–5pm, Thu until 9pm | admission C$14 | 130 9th Ave. SE*

### HERITAGE PARK HISTORICAL VILLAGE
On the shores of the Glenmore reservoir this reconstructed pioneer village and open-air museum depicts life in the Canadian 'Wild West'. There is also a steam train and paddle steamer. *Daily in summer 9:30am–5pm, spring and autumn*

*only Sat/Sun | admission C$20 | 1900 heritage Dr. SW*

## CITY CENTRE

Walk from Calgary Tower through the city centre to the *Devonian Gardens (7th Ave. | 3rd St.)*, a large park and botanical garden enclosed in glass at the top of a shopping mall. Just north on Centre Street is the small *Chinatown* and the *Chinese Cultural Centre (197 1st St.)*. East of that, on the banks of the Bow River, are the foundations of the *Fort Calgary* police post (now a visitor centre).

## FOOD & DRINK

### EAU CLAIRE MARKET

Popular restaurants and bars ensure throngs of visitors to this shopping centre, such as *Bow River Barley Mill,* the trendy *Joey Tomatoes* and the pool bar *The Garage.* The historic *1886 Buffalo Cafe* on the western side of the market is also very pleasant.

### THE PALOMINO

Rustic BBQ restaurant and bar serving hearty Tex-Mex fare; INSIDER TIP in the evening they often have live rock or country music in the basement. *109 7th Ave. SW | tel. 403 5 32 19 11 | Budget–Moderate*

### THE TRIBUNE

Excellent steakhouse with traditional wood décor. Also very good lamb. *100 8th Ave. SW | tel. 403 2 69 31 60 | Expensive*

## SHOPPING

Western clothes, cowboy boots and Stetsons are without doubt the most popular souvenirs from Calgary. You will find the best selection at INSIDER TIP *Alberta Boot (50 50th Ave. SE)* and *Lammle's Western Wear* in the *Heritage Store* at the *Stephen Avenue Mall,* along the many more shopping malls.

## CROSSIRON MILLS ●

Huge shopping centre on the northern edge of Calgary with approximately 200 stores, there are also often discount sales. *Daily 10am–9pm, Sun to 6pm | 261055 Crossiron Blvd., Hwy. 2 north of the airport | www.deerfootmall.ca*

## RIVA'S ECO STORE ☺

Everything you buy in this trendy shop on the eastern edge of the city centre is organic and eco-friendly: cosmetics, shoes, clothes, furniture. *1237 9th Ave. SE | www.rivasecostore.com*

## SPORTS & ACTIVITIES

### CALGARY MILLENNIUM PARK

The world's largest skate park is at the western end of the city centre. Almost 2 acres

---

MARCO POLO HIGHLIGHTS

★ **Ranchman's Saloon**
Steaks and country music – the Wild West lives on! → p. 84

★ **Royal Tyrrell Museum of Palaeontology**
Just north of Drumheller, the museum has massive dinosaurs displayed in a primeval landscape → p. 85

★ **West Edmonton Mall**
The largest shopping centre in North America → p. 86

★ **Head-Smashed-In Buffalo Jump**
Where the Blackfoot Indians drove herds of bison over the cliff → p. 87

of pipes, stairs, jumps and ramps that is open to the public around the clock. *1220 9th Ave. SW*

## ENTERTAINMENT

Many bars, restaurants and dance clubs are along 17th Avenue SW between 4th and 8th Street. All Country & Western music fans should visit the ★ ● *Ranchman's Saloon (9615 Macleod Trail S)*, where – according to their advertising – all the real cowboys meet (live music on weekdays at 7pm) INSIDER TIP free two-step and line dancing lessons. If you don't want to drive far there is also the *Roadhouse (840 9th Ave.) SW)*, on the outskirts of the city centre, a popular music club with country music evenings. Jazz fans should try *Beat Niq (811 1st. St. SW)*.

## WHERE TO STAY

### ECONOLODGE
Well-maintained chain of motels, this one is located close to the Trans-Canada Highway. *56 rooms | 2440 16Th Ave. NW | tel. 403 2 89 25 61 | www.econolodgecalgary. com | Budget*

### FOUR POINTS SHERATON
A modern hotel on the western edge of the city near the Olympic Park. *150 rooms | 8220 Bowridge Crescent NW | tel. 403 2 88 44 41 | www.fourpointscalgarywest.com | Moderate*

### KENSINGTON RIVERSIDE INN
Elegant, small luxury hotel on the Bow River near the city centre. *19 rooms | 1126 Memorial Dr. NW | tel. 403 2 28 44 42 | www. kensingtonriversideinn.com | Expensive*

## INFORMATION

### TOURISM CALGARY
Information kiosks at the airport and in the Calgary Tower. *238 11th Ave. SW | Calgary | tel. 403 2 63 85 10 | www.visit calgary.com*

## WHERE TO GO

### INSIDER TIP BLACKFOOT CROSSING HISTORICAL PARK 🕓
(135 D5) (*∅ J14*)
In the middle of the prairies about 130km/ 80mi east of Calgary is the newly built eco-friendly cultural centre of the Black-foot Indians. The performances and exhibitions include dances, archaeological excavations, and tepee accommodation

# LOW BUDGET

▶ The *Olympic Plaza* on the east side of the city centre *(200 8th Ave.)* is a legacy of the 1988 Olympic Games in Calgary and today it hosts free lunchtime concerts in the summer and in winter the Plaza is a free ice skating rink.

▶ The Edmonton tourist office website offers discounted coupons for museum entrance fees and special offers: *www.edmonton.com.* You can find also information about the many concerts and festivals hosted by the city. Tickets are available at short notice from *Tix on the Square (9930 102nd Ave. NW)*.

▶ Do some advance planning and it will pay off: if you go to British Columbia, you should shop in Alberta. There is no provincial tax, across the border the tax is 7 per cent. Wine and other alcohol is cheaper in Alberta.

A must for dinosaur and fossil enthusiasts: Royal Tyrrell Museum of Palaeontology in Drumheller

and guided tours. The location of the cultural centre also has special meaning: this was where the Prairie tribes signed the treaty with the whites that gave up their land in 1877. *Daily in summer 9am–5pm | admission C$10 | Hwy. 842 | Siksika | www.blackfootcrossing.ca*

### DRUMHELLER (135 D4) *(ⓜ J13)*

About 140km/87mi north-east of Calgary are the *Alberta badlands* – a bizarre barren landscape weathered by erosion – of the Red Deer River. A drive along the 54km/33mi *Dinosaur Trail* shows multicoloured alluvial fans of deposits and strange rock pillars, where many fossils have already been discovered. The most impressive finds of the dinosaurs that inhabited this region, some 65 million years ago, are housed in the ★ ● *Royal Tyrrell Museum of Palaeontology (in the summer 9am–9pm, otherwise Tue–Sun 10am–5pm | admission C$11 | www.tyrrellmuseum.com)*. The perfectly staged exhibits bring prehistory to life and include well known ones such as

Tyrannosaurus Rex through to lesser known ones such as dinosaurs with webbed feet. *www.traveldrumheller.com*

# EDMONTON

(135 D3) *(ⓜ J12)* **From the fur trading era to the gold rush and the oil boom – the provincial capital of Alberta developed from a village to a metropolis of 1.1 million inhabitants.**

In addition to the government, the oil industry is the main supplier of jobs. However, there is little sign of the oil industry in the city itself. Its straight streets, neatly laid out in checkerboard style, are lined with manicured neighbourhoods while glass and steel office towers are springing up in the city centre. From a tourist perspective, Edmonton with its international airport is mainly a springboard for trips to the Rockies and – via the Alaska Highway and Mackenzie Highway – to the far north of Canada.

The West Edmonton Mall is both a shopping and entertainment centre

## SIGHTSEEING

### FORT EDMONTON PARK
The extensive open-air museum depicts the city's history from its fur trading days up to the 20th century. The 1845 Hudson's Bay Company fort has been reconstructed true to detail. *Daily in summer 10am–6pm | admission C$15.75 | Whitemud Freeway*

### CITY CENTRE
The modern city centre is on a hill overlooking the scenic North Saskatchewan River valley fringed by numerous large parks. All the action is around the vibrant *Sir Winston Churchill Square* with its art galleries and theatres. The main shopping street is the parallel running *Jasper Avenue*.

### MUTTART CONSERVATORY
Botanical garden on the riverbank with four futuristic glass pyramids – different ecosystems – make an impressive accent against the urban skyline of the city centre. *Daily 10am–5pm | admission C$11.75 | 9626 96A St.*

### ROYAL ALBERTA MUSEUM
Pioneer history, Native American culture and dinosaurs. Large temporary exhibitions. *Daily 9am–5pm | admission C$11 | 12845 102nd Ave.*

## FOOD & DRINK

### BLUE PLATE DINNER ☺
A modern bistro with local art on the walls, serving creative organic food. *10145 104 St. | tel. 780 4 29 07 40 | Moderate*

### RIC'S GRILL
A casual restaurant in the city centre, serving steak and fish dishes. Good bar with tapas. *10190 104th St. | tel. 780 4 29 43 33 | Moderate*

## SHOPPING

### WEST EDMONTON MALL ★
The largest shopping mall in North America is both a shopper's paradise and an attraction. Here you will find more than 800 shops and restaurants, a large amusement park, an artificial lake (with submarines!)

and even a wave pool – all under one roof. You just have to see it for yourself! *87th Ave./170th St. | www.wem.ca*

## ENTERTAINMENT

Night owls will be at home in the university district of *Old Strathcona* on the south bank of the Saskatchewan. Around *82nd Avenue* (known here as *Whyte Avenue*) are numerous cafés, restaurants and music venues. Country & Western music fans should head for *Cook County Saloon (8010 103rd St.)* while jazz lovers will enjoy the live bands in the *Yardbird Suite (102nd St./86th Ave.)*.

## WHERE TO STAY

### FANTASY LAND
A hotel so kitsch you have to see it to believe it: more than 120 of the 355 rooms are styled according to different themes – Arabic, Hollywood, Igloo or Polynesia and so on. *17700 87th Ave. | tel. 780 4 44 30 00 | www.fantasylandhotel.com | Expensive*

### ROYAL INN
Comfortable mid range hotel near West Edmonton Mall, with a pleasant bistro. *236 rooms | 10010 178th St. | tel. 888 3 88 39 32 | www.executivehotels.net | Budget–Moderate*

## INFORMATION

### EDMONTON TOURISM
*9990 Jasper Ave. | tel. 800 4 63 46 67 | www.edmonton.com*

## WHERE TO GO

### ELK ISLAND NATIONAL PARK
(135 D3) (*∅ J12*)
The fenced, 77 square mile park is about 40km/25mi east of Edmonton and pro-

vides a protected habitat for a large herd of Plains bison, moose, Wapiti deer and more than 200 species of birds.

### REYNOLDS-ALBERTA MUSEUM
(135 D3) (*∅ J12*)
About 60km/37mi south, the museum traces the mechanisation of Alberta's transportation with historical farming equipment, airplanes, cars etc. *Daily in the summer 10am–5pm, otherwise Tue–Thu 10am–5pm | admission C$10 | Wetaskiwin Hwy. 13*

# FORT MACLEOD

(135 D6) (*∅ J14*) **This small farming village (pop. 3000) on the Oldman River in southern Alberta prairie is one of the oldest settlements in western Canada.** As early as 1874 the *Northwest Mounted Police* founded here a fort to curb the whiskey trade with the Native Americans – the first outpost in the Wild West.

## SIGHTSEEING

### INSIDER TIP THE FORT MUSEUM OF THE NORTH WEST MOUNTED POLICE
In the (reconstructed) police fort, students in the historical uniforms of the Canadian police perform riding demonstrations. *In summer daily 9am–6pm, otherwise 9am–5pm | admission C$12, low season C$10 | 25th St./3rd Ave | www.nwmpmuseum.com*

### HEAD-SMASHED-IN BUFFALO JUMP ★
Name says it all: this was where the Native Americans drove herds of bison over a cliff. The women waited below to carve the animals and dry the meat for winter provisions. The excellent museum nearly *20km/12.5mi west of Fort Macleod in the*

Blackfoot Indian reservation details the lifestyle and hunting methods of the Plains Indians. *Daily in the summer 9am–6pm, otherwise 10am–5pm | admission C$10 | Hwy. 785 | history.alberta.ca*

# FORT MCMURRAY

(135 E1) *(⌀ J–K10)* **Out in the wilderness of northern Alberta, the city (pop. 60,000) is an oil production hub. It is estimated that there are 27 billion tons of oil in the tar sands below the city.**
In the 1960s an oil plant was opened here in the midst of the endless forest and from this a city boomed. Those interested in technology can visit the state of the art *Oil Sands Discovery Centre (daily in the summer 9am–5pm, otherwise Tue–Sun 10am–4pm | admission C$7).*

# LETHBRIDGE

(135 D6) *(⌀ J14)* **The farming town (pop. 84,000) is the most important city in southern Alberta.**
In the *Indian Battle Park* on the western edge of the city is the notorious pioneer trading post *Fort Whoop-up,* where American whiskey traders cheated the Native Americans by trading highly over-priced whiskey for their pelts *(July/August daily 10am–5pm, otherwise Mon/Tue closed).* Somewhat out of place in the prairie – but very interesting – is the *Nikko Yuko Japanese Gardens* in Henderson Park, a manicured park in the traditional Japanese style *(May–Oct 9am–8pm).*

## WHERE TO GO

### WRITING-ON-STONE PROV. PARK
(135 D6) *(⌀ J15)*
The main attraction of the park, in the valley of the Milk River south of Lethbridge, are the hoodoos, oddly shaped stone pillars formed by wind and weather. The region was sacred to the Native Americans, and they left behind many petroglyphs. *In summer daily guided tours | tel. 403 6 47 23 64 to make a reservation*

# MEDICINE HAT

(135 E5) *(⌀ K14)* **The largest city in south-eastern Alberta (pop. 57,000) depends largely on the natural gas industry,**

# ENCOUNTERING BEARS

Your chances of getting a photo of a bear are not bad: black bears are practically everywhere – sniffing around campsites or taking a leisurely saunter along the highway. Unlike the shy grizzly bears – which you will only encounter in the hinterland in the Rocky Mountains – or the extremely dangerous (and powerful) polar bears that live near the Arctic. But while black bears look very cute you have to exercise caution: remember to keep your distance when photographing them, store your food at night in the car when camping, and immediately wash your dishes after eating.

The hoodoos in the Writing-On-Stone Provincial Park were shaped by the weather

**is a major stop on the Trans-Canada Highway, as well as a supply centre for the farms in the surrounding district.**

The strange sounding name of the town probably originates during the time of conflict between the Blackfoot and Cree Indians – a medicine man of the Cree lost his headdress in battle and his tribesmen interpreted this as a bad omen resulting in a bloody defeat.

## WHERE TO GO

### CYPRESS HILLS PROV. PARK
(135 E5–6) (*K14*)

Cypress Hills looms out of the prairies 100km/62m south-east of Medicine Hat – a green oasis in the vast plains. In the ice ages, the region was not covered in glaciers and so the prairie developed its unusual vegetation. In *Loch Leven* you can rent canoes and bicycles. An accommodation tip is the *Historic Reesor Ranch,* an original, century old ranch just beyond the border with Saskatchewan, where guests stay in four B & B rooms and two log cabins *(Walsh | tel. 306 6 62 34 98 | www.reesor ranch.com | Budget)*.

### DINOSAUR PROV. PARK
(135 E5) (*K14*)

The river bed of the Red Deer River, about 200km/124mi north-west, is one of the best dinosaur fossils sites worldwide. 35 species of dinosaur have already been discovered here and Unesco has declared the region a World Heritage Site. There are nature trails and bus tours to the archaeological sites and the visitor centre exhibits a selection of the finds. Fossil enthusiasts who want to stay over will be enjoy *Comfort Camping (7 tents | May–Oct tel. 403 3 78 43 44 | albertaparks.ca/dinosaur.aspx | Budget–Moderate)* on the banks of the Red Deer River where all the equipment – including proper beds – is included.

# NORTHERN CANADA

For wilderness enthusiasts and nature lovers, the region north of the 60th parallel is the most spectacular part of Canada. It is a raw, largely untouched land, whose austere beauty provides ample material for tales of trappers, prospectors, and lost expeditions.

The northern massive region is massive and comprises about a third of Canada's total area. Politically, the north is divided into three territories: the mountainous Yukon in the west (which experienced the largest gold rush of all time about 100 years ago in the Klondike), the Northwest Territories, stretching around the huge Mackenzie River Valley and the Great Slave Lake, and the Nunavut Territory (established in 1999) which extends from Hudson Bay to the North Pole. Only about 35,000 people live in the Yukon, 75,000 in the Northwest Territories and Nunavut, which is predominantly inhabited and governed by the Inuit. The Northwest Territories are home to the Dene Indians who are now also demanding their own an independent region. Good equipment and careful planning are essential for a trip into northern Canada, even when it is nice and warm in the summer (30°C/86°F). The easiest travel is in the region around the Great Slave Lake and in the Yukon, where there are roads and a tour-

Photo: On the Dempster Highway

**In the footsteps of Jack London: on the backcountry roads of the far north you will often not see another soul for hours**

ist infrastructure. The most important routes in the north are the Alaska Highway and the Mackenzie Highway from Edmonton to Yellowknife on the Great Slave Lake. From there the roads leading into the hinterland are only gravel tracks: the Liard Highway to the Nahanni National Park, the Klondike Highway to the historic gold rush area – brought to life by the stories of Jack London – around Dawson City. All the other Arctic regions can only be reached by aircraft.

# DAWSON CITY

(126 A5) *(∅ B4)* ★ ● **The gold rush era lives on in this practically deserted ghost town, once known as the 'Paris of the North'.**

The French cancan has entertained the gold miners in Dawson City for more than 100 years

About 30,000 people lived here during the Klondike gold rush in the 1900s, and the town at the mouth of the Klondike River in the Yukon is now a Historic Site characterised by Wild West sidewalks and wooden facades. There are only around 2000 inhabitants in Dawson City today; their income is mainly from tourism, but the current high price of gold has once again drawn miners to the surrounding goldfields. For the most beautiful views follow the gravel road up to the 1000m/3280ft high lookout point ☀ *Midnight Dome*.

## SIGHTSEEING

### DAWSON CITY MUSEUM

The museum documents the gold rush era of the town with historical photos, mining equipment and mining tools. Also film screenings and gold washing demonstrations. *Daily in summer 10am–6pm | admission C$10 | 5th Ave./Church St.*

### HISTORIC DISTRICT

Cancan girls high kick in *Diamond Tooth Gertie's Gambling Hall*, there are performances and guided tours of the *Palace Grand Theatre* are listed, and in *Jack London's cabin* there are photos, documents and letters that bring to life his novels. Many of the renovated old buildings are open to the public, such as the old post office on King Street, the elegant *Commissioner's residence* (guides) on Front Street, as well as the historic paddle steamer, the *SS Keno* on the banks of the Yukon River.

## FOOD & DRINK

### KLONDIKE KATE'S

Cosy pub in historic building with a terrace. Great menu selection and good coffee. *3rd Ave./King St. | tel. 867 9 93 65 27 | Moderate*

## WHERE TO STAY

### BOMBAY PEGGY'S

The former brothel is now a comfortable guest house but they still have INSIDER TIP a good pub. *9 rooms | Princess St./ 2nd Ave. | Phone 867 9 93 69 69 | www. bombaypeggys.com | Moderate*

### ELDORADO

The 52 rooms are modern and comfortable, but not very luxurious. With restaurant and saloon. *3rd Ave./Princess St. | tel. 867 9 93 54 51 | www.eldoradohotel.ca | Moderate*

## INFORMATION

### VISITOR RECEPTION CENTRE

The visitor centre also organises slide shows and guided tours of the city. *Front St./King St. | tel. 867 9 93 55 66 | www. dawsoncity.ca*

## WHERE TO GO

### BONANZA CREEK (126 A5) *(Ø B4)*

In 1896 the first gold was discovered here 5km/3mi south, in the valley of the Klondike River. Two Historic Sites, a mining claim and a preserved sluice dredge, *Dredge No. 4,* testify to the rigors of the gold prospectors.

### DEMPSTER HIGHWAY ★ ●
(126 A–C 2–5) *(Ø B–D 2–4)*

This gravel road runs over 700km/435mi from Dawson City to the deserted tundra regions north of the Arctic Circle to the Inuit settlement of *Inuvik* in the Mackenzie Delta. There are only two tiny Native American villages and a petrol station along the entire route; otherwise there is nothing but the Arctic wilderness. The highway, which was completed in 1959, is especially scenic in early September when autumn transforms the foliage into a sea of colour.

### TOP OF THE WORLD HIGHWAY/
### TAYLOR HIGHWAY ⚜
(126 A5) *(Ø A–B4)*

The most scenic stretch is the 270km/ 168mi section from the Yukon to Alaska – a panoramic ride through isolated mountain peaks, verdant valleys and old gold mining areas. There is only one place along the way, the old mining hamlet of *Chicken* in Alaska. At *Tok* Highway 9 connects to the Alaska Highway making a round trip back to Whitehorse possible. *(Road only open from late May–Sept)*

# HAINES JUNCTION

(128 B2) *(Ø B6)* **The tiny, hill fringed village where the Alaska Highway meets the Haines Highway, is a good starting point for trips to the Kluane National Park. The park covers 8495 square miles of pristine mountain wilderness in the westernmost corner of the Yukon.**

This is where you will find Canada's highest peak, *Mount Logan* in the ice-covered St. Elias Mountains on the border to Alaska.

---

★ **Dawson City**
The gold rush city in the Klondike is still a bustling little town → p. 91

★ **Dempster Highway**
The famed wilderness road runs from Dawson City up into the Mackenzie Delta → p. 93

★ **SS Klondike**
An original paddle steamer from the good old gold rush days of yore → p. 95

★ **Prince of Wales Northern Heritage Centre**
Preserving pioneer history and indigenous cultures → p. 96

**MARCO POLO HIGHLIGHTS**

---

The Alaska Highway runs along the northern edge of the park (slideshow in the visitor centre) on the banks of the 150 square mile large *Kluane Lake* where trails lead into the foothills of the *Kluane Range*. In the east of the park is *Kathleen Lake,* a beautiful hiking region.

The northern lights in Inuvik are best seen in the winter

The ❄️ *Kluane B & B (8 rooms | tel. 867 8 41 42 50 | Alaska Hwy., 55km/34mi west of Haines Junction | www.kluanecabins. com | Budget)* offers rustic cabins, great pancake breakfasts and a spectacular location on the shores of Kluane Lake. *Paddle Wheel Adventures (tel. 867 6 34 26 83 | www.paddlewheeladventures.com)* rent out mountain bikes and canoes, and also offer sightseeing flights, rafting, and guided hikes.

# INUVIK

**(126 C2) (∅ D2) About 3000 people (Inuit, Dene, and other cultures) live here on the eastern edge of the vast Mackenzie Delta and lives up to its name of 'Place of the People'.**
After the 700km/435mi long ride on the *Dempster Highway* from Dawson City, you deserve a few sightseeing flights over the area, such as to the remote trapper village of *Aklavik* in the middle of the 80km/50mi wide river delta, to the old whaling station on *Herschel Island*, or to the Inuit settlement of *Tuktoyaktuk* on the Arctic Ocean coast. Trips such as these can be organised by, for example, *White Husky Tours (tel. 867 7 77 35 35 | www.whitehuskies.com)* who also run a log cabin B & B and breed sled dogs.

# WATSON LAKE

**(129 D–E3) (∅ D7) Since the construction of the Alaska Highway in 1942 the village (pop. 800) in the southern Yukon has become an important supply base.**
It is also home to the *Watson Lake Signpost Forest,* with signposts from all over the world, started 50 years ago by a homesick soldier. Next to it is a modern *Interpretive Centre* that details the history of the Alaska Highway.

## WHERE TO GO

MUNCHO LAKE **(129 E3) (∅ E8)**
The 11km/7mi long emerald green lake lies about 300km/187mi miles south-

east on the Alaska Highway (in British Columbia). Stop off at the *Liard River Hot Springs Park* and soak away the dust of the wilderness.

The INSIDER TIP *Northern Rockies Lodge (45 rooms, 10 cabins | Mile 462 | tel. 250 7 76 34 81 | www.northernrockieslodge. com | Moderate)* offers rooms on the shores of the lake and air safaris into the Nahanni Park.

### NAHANNI NAT. PARK
(129 E–F 1–2) (*ℳ EF 6–7*)

The park is an hour's flight north-east of Watson Lake and is a popular white water rafting destination: the *South Nahanni River* runs through the *Mackenzie Mountains* before thundering over the 90m/ 300ft high *Virginia Falls* and into deep gorges. In Whitehorse companies such as *Nahanni River Adventures (tel. 867 6 68 31 80 | www.nahanni.com)* offers guided canoe trips and wilderness expeditions.

# WHITEHORSE

(128 C2) (*ℳ B–C6*) **The Yukon's bustling capital (pop. 24,000) stretches out along the broad bank of the Yukon River.**

The city's heyday was as a transport hub around 1900, when thousands of prospectors arrived on crudely build rafts and boats through the hazardous *Miles Canyon,* on their way to the gold fields of the Klondike. You can learn more about its golden era in the *MacBride Museum* and in the *Old Log Church Museum.*

## SIGHTSEEING

### SS KLONDIKE ⭐
Built in 1937, the historic paddle steamer has been lovingly restored and is now open to the public; it is on dry land on the

banks of the Yukon River. *Daily 9.30am– 5pm | admission C$6 | 2nd Ave.*

## TOURS

A good resource is the *Wilderness Tourism Association* website that lists more than 20 adventure companies: *www.yukon wild.com.*

### KANOE PEOPLE ●
Here you will get all the equipment for a leisurely canoe trip on the Yukon to Dawson City including canoes, tents, etc.

# LOW BUDGET

▶ On the quiet west side of the Yukon River is the northernmost hostel in Canada, the *Dawson City River Hostel (Dawson City | tel. 867 9 93 68 23 | www.yukonhostels.com).* Accommodation costs C$14–22 and is in simple log cabins or there are also campsites. Only open in the summer.

▶ The alternative crowd, motor home travellers and canoeists: this is the clientele at the ☺ *Alpine Bakery (411 Alexander St. | tel. 867 6 68 68 71 | www.alpinebakery.ca)* in Whitehorse where you can get very reasonably priced caffè latte, healthy muffins and organic bread for your trip into the hinterland.

▶ For only C$6.30 you can relive the gold rush era: twice daily an actor reads from works such as 'The Spell of the Yukon'. Very atmospheric. *Robert Service Cabin | ask for times at the visitors bureau | 8th Ave. | Dawson City*

Guided tours are also offered. *1147 First Ave. | tel. 867 6 68 48 99 | www.kanoe people.com*

## FOOD & DRINK

### KLONDIKE RIB & SALMON BBQ
Rustic restaurant in an old pioneer cabin; good chowder, salmon and ribs. *2116 2nd Ave. | tel. 867 6 67 75 54 | Expensive*

### JARVIS STREET SALOON
Large saloon serving burgers and pub meals, it draws the younger crowd and there are often live bands in the evening. *206 Jarvis St. | tel. 867 6 68 45 67 | www. saloononjarvis.com | Budget*

## WHERE TO STAY

### HIGH COUNTRY INN
Centrally located with a very popular **INSIDER TIP** terrace bar and BBQ grill: *The Deck. 85 rooms | 405 14th Ave. | tel. 867 6 67 44 71 | www.highcountryinn.yk.ca | Moderate*

### HISTORICAL GUEST HOUSE
Cosy, simple accommodation, in the city centre with a very helpful host. *3 rooms | 5128 5th Ave. | tel. 867 6 68 39 07 | www. yukongold.com | Budget–Moderate*

### INN ON THE LAKE
An idyllic cabin style lodge in a quiet location on Marsh Lake, with superb cuisine. *15 rooms | Alaska Hwy. 35mins drive from Whitehorse | tel. 867 6 60 52 53 | www.exceptionalplaces.com | Moderate– Expensive*

## INFORMATION

### TOURISM YUKON
*Hanson St./2nd Ave. | Whitehorse | tel. 867 6 67 53 40 | www.travelyukon.com*

## WHERE TO GO

**INSIDER TIP** ATLIN ☼
(128 C3) *(ꕤ B–C7)*
Atlin is well worth the roughly 170km/ 105mi drive south due to its magnificent location, surrounded by mountains on the shores of Atlin Lake. The picturesque, weathered gold mining village (founded in 1898 during the Klondike gold rush) is actually in British Columbia but is only accessible from the Yukon. Today, around 500 people live in and around Atlin: gold prospectors, artists, dropouts. One thing you must do is to take a scenic flight over the glacier covered Coast Mountains with *Atlin Air Charters (tel. 250 6 51 00 25)*. Or take a boat or hiking trip deep into the region's untouched hinterland with *Atlin Quest (tel. 250 6 51 74 52 | www.atlinquest. com)*.

# YELLOWKNIFE

(131 D2) *(ꕤ J6)* **The best views over the modern capital of the Northwest Territories are from the** ☼ *Pilot's Monument* **on a bare rock outcrop.**
The 17,000 inhabitants are either state employees or involved in the two gold mines. In 1990 diamonds were discovered north of the city, and they now also have their first diamond mine.

## SIGHTSEEING

### PRINCE OF WALES NORTHERN HERITAGE CENTRE ★
Without a doubt the best museum in the North West Territories. The museum has exhibits about the flora and fauna of the Arctic and Yellowknife is a great place to see the northern lights. *Daily in the summer 10.30am–5pm | admission free | Frame Lake St./48th St.*

## FOOD & DRINK/ WHERE TO STAY

### BATHURST INLET LODGE ☺

An eco wilderness lodge on the Arctic Sea coast, for wildlife watching and tundra exploration. Access by chartered flights from Yellowknife – book well in advance! *10 rooms | tel. 867 8 73 25 95 | www. bathurstinletlodge.com | Expensive*

### BAYSIDE B & B ⊰⊱

Accommodation in a large wooden house on the shore of Great Slave Lake, with a

## INFORMATION

**NORTHWEST TERRITORIES TOURISM**
*Visitor centres at the airport and 4807 49th St. | Yellowknife | tel. 867 8 73 72 00 | www.spectacularnwt.com*

## WHERE TO GO

### WOOD BUFFALO NAT. PARK
(131 D–E 3–5) (*ᗰ H–J8*)

With 17,500 square miles the reserve in the delta of the Peace and Athabasca rivers is the largest national park in Canada. The

In the Wood Buffalo National Park the bison herd is over 3000 animals strong

popular restaurant. *5 rooms | 3505 McDonald Dr. | tel. 867 6 69 88 44 | www. baysidenorth.com | Budget–Moderate*

### THE WILDCAT CAFÉ

An institution: hearty pioneer kitchen and caribou steaks. *3904 Wylie Rd. | tel. 867 8 73 88 50 | Moderate*

endless forests are home to 3000 wild bison while the wetlands are home to numerous water birds, including rare cranes and white pelicans.
Some gravel tracks lead from the *Fort Smith (visitor centre)* into the reserve and you can also take a cruise on the Slave River.

# TRIPS & TOURS

The tours are marked in green in the road atlas, the pull-out map and on the back cover

**1** PRAIRIES, MOUNTAINS AND LAKES: FROM EAST TO WEST

An introductory tour (8–10 days) that is ideal for first time visitors. You will experience the diversity of western Canada's nature from the Calgary prairies to the ice-capped peaks of the Rockies and from the wooded lake district, in the interior of British Columbia, to the Pacific Coast in Vancouver. And there is time for hikes or other activities along the way. Combine the drive with the following routes for a long tour. The best time to do the 1500km/930mi route is in the warmer months from June to early October.

Calgary → p. 81 deserves a stay of at least a day, to visit the museums and to go shopping in the modern malls. But then you head off westwards into the vast country: the Trans-Canada Highway leads along the Bow River through the old tribal prairie lands of the Blackfoot Indians to the mountains. At Canmore the mountains draw closer to Highway 1 which leads – right after the first sign warning about bears – to the entrance of Banff National Park → p. 67, the oldest and most famous reserve in the Rockies. Plan on at least two nights in Banff or Lake

On the trail of fur trappers and traders: explore western Canada with the best routes by car, ferry or on hikes along the coast

Louise so that you have time to go hiking in the mountains, either to Moraine Lake or to Johnstone Canyon. From Lake Louise you can make a detour to the lesser known Yoho National Park → p. 78, where the highest waterfalls in the Rockies, the Takakkaw Falls, are fed by melt water from the Waputik Icefield.

Next you head further northwards with a drive on the ☆☆ Icefields Parkway → p. 69 and you should keep your camera ready as the scenery is spectacular, especially the narrow gorge of the Mistaya River and the magnificent panoramic view at Waterfowl Lake. After the steep climb to the 2035m/6677ft Sunwapta Pass the two hour INSIDER TIP *Parker Ridge Trail* is recommended (but only in good weather) before continuing the route to the Athabasca Glacier → p. 73

in Jasper National Park → p. 73. Here you can take another break and go for a hike in the Maligne Canyon → p. 74 and a boat trip on Maligne Lake. Highway 16 heads westwards over the border to British Columbia (time zone is minus 1 hour). With a little luck it will be sunny and you will be able to see the ice-capped summit of the highest peak in the Rockies, Mount Robson → p. 75.

The next leg of the trip is through the completely undeveloped mountainous regions on the western flank of the Rockies and runs from Valemount (in winter a heli-skiing centre) southwards on Highway 5. Towns and filling stations are only available every 70km/40mi or so along this stretch. After a detour to the waterfalls in the equally isolated Wells Gray Provincial Park → p. 62 you will once again reach civilisation in the ranch country around Kamloops → p. 55. The Trans-Canada Highway then winds further west in the Thompson River valley. Here in the 'interior' of BC it is almost as dry as a desert, countryside straight out of a Western. A visit to INSIDER TIP Hat Creek Ranch in Cache Creek: a faithfully preserved stagecoach station (May–Sept daily 9am–5pm | admission C$12) is very fitting given the environment. Even more pioneer history awaits in Lillooet, a classic pioneer town at the beginning of the Cariboo Road, the old gold rush route. Tip: the Lillooet Bakery (717 Main St.) has a delicious selection of treats including apple strudel.

From Lillooet the route follows the Fraser River – that has carved a deep canyon through the Coast Mountains – to the sea. The narrowest and wildest section lies south of Lytton → p. 56. Dense forests cover the mountain slopes and accompany Highway 1 through the widening Fraser Valley up to the end of the journey in Vancouver → p. 32.

## 2 HEADING SOUTH: FORESTS AND TRANQUIL LAKES

The sunny south of the provinces offers holiday enjoyment in Wild West hamlets and elongated lakes. There is no shortage of attractions for nature lovers as there are national parks (such as Waterton Lakes), museum villages (such as Fort Steele) and ghost towns from the gold rush era all along on the way. You should set aside about 10 days to cover the nearly 1900km/1180mi long route.

From Vancouver → p. 32 the route goes eastwards to the broad, fertile Fraser Valley. To set the tone of the trip into pioneer country, make a stop at the museum village of Fort Langley → p. 39, where the fur trader era is brought back to life. From the village of Hope, Highway 3 climbs up the Coast Mountains to the wooded Manning Provincial Park, where rhododendrons bloom in the wild in spring and where there are some hiking trails. The 1346m/4416ft high Allison Pass then descends into the dry, sunny eastern side of the mountains in the valley of the Similkameen River. Orchards line the valley floor and farmers sell cherries and peaches at street stalls along the way.

Osoyoos is located close to the US border and the long beaches of Osoyoos Lake give it the feeling of a Mediterranean resort. The route now goes northward to the Okanagan Valley → p. 58 passing sandy beaches, orchards and vineyards. North of Vernon the Trans-Canada Highway soon becomes lonely and quiet. Deep in the woods of the Monashee Mountains there is Craigellachie and the historic railway station where the last spike was driven into the Trans-Canada Railway on 9 November 1885.

If it is summer then you should treat yourself to the wild flower meadows in the Mount Revelstoke National Park → p. 57. Thereafter the route continues on Highway 23, 31 and 3A southwards to the Arrow Lakes → p. 58 region. Untouched pioneer country with scattered small villages, beautiful provincial parks set in mountainous wilderness and long stretches of lakes that are serviced by car ferries.

The route continues (time zone plus 1 hour) again near the US border, to Cranbrook (with a large railway museum) and the museum village Fort Steele at Kimberley → p. 76. In the east the peaks of the Rocky Mountains rise up where Highway 3 crosses the Crowsnest Pass → p. 73 at a height of 1396m/4580ft. The Frank Slide Visitor Centre depicts the hard lives of miners at the end of the 19th century.

Profusion of wild flowers on the summit of Mount Revelstoke in the eponymous national park

Worthwhile stops along the way include the hot springs at Nakusp and Ainsworth, the small ghost town of Sandon that dates back to the silver boom around 1890 and the picturesque old mining village Nelson. In the Kokanee Creek Provincial Park you can watch the salmon spawning in August. An accommodation tip is the historic *Willow Point Lodge (7 rooms | 2211 Taylor Dr. | tel. 250 8 25 94 11 | www.willow pointlodge.com | Moderate–Expensive)* set in lush gardens.

At Pincher Creek the highway heads out into the endless prairie – but first a detour to the south, to the sublime mountain scenery of the Waterton Lakes National Park → p. 77, where boat trips and hiking trails await. Thereafter the route leaves the mountains and heads to Fort Macleod → p. 87, with its excellent Native American museum, and further northwards through the ranch country of Alberta to the end point of the tour, Calgary → p. 81, Canada's oil capital.

## THE WEST COAST: FJORDS AND VERDANT ISLANDS

**This route traces the rugged Pacific coastline along the famous Inside Passage and explores the wilderness of** northern British Columbia – a journey into the realm of the Native Americans, lumberjacks and pioneer farmers. The route is 2400km/1490mi (excluding ferry trips) and the time required is approx. 14 days. It is important to remember that the ferry ride from Port Hardy to Prince Rupert must be booked in advance.

Car ferries to Vancouver Island depart every hour from Tsawwassen on the southern edge of Vancouver → p. 32. From here it is not far to Victoria → p. 47, with its excellent provincial museum and charming old town. Set aside at least a day to explore the town.

Then the trip continues via the Trans-Canada Highway to the Goldstream Park just on the outskirts of town. In late autumn the salmon run upstream to their spawning grounds and then die in the shallow water – an impressive spectacle of nature. About a day ride further – past bathing beaches and tourist resorts such as Chemainus, famous for its 30 large murals by international artists – it is off to the western coast of Vancouver Island and the Pacific Rim National Park → p. 44. The fishing village Tofino is the best place to take a break for a day to enjoy walks on the beach, a cruise or kayak ride. Back on the eastern coast, the route then goes via Campbell River → p. 41 on Highway 19 to the north of Vancouver Island. Not to be missed: whale watching excursion from Telegraph Cove → p. 46 and a detour to Alert Bay → p. 46, where there is a beautiful collection of totem poles and Native American masks. The next morning your journey continues from Port Hardy → p. 46 by ferry through the Inside Passage → p. 46 and with a little luck the sun may shine. It normally rains here, because the steep slopes of the Coast Mountains trap the Pacific clouds. But this also has its advantages and the stretch of coast is a unique jungle of towering Douglas firs and Sitka spruces. You may also spot whales, seals and bald eagles.

About 15 hours later you will reach Prince Rupert → p. 65. The ferry port at the northern end of the Inside Passage is in the realm of the Tsimshian Indians. Everywhere in the town there are large totem poles and carvings. In Port Edward the North Pacific Cannery (July/Aug 9.30am–5pm, in the spring and autumn Mon closed | admission C$12) represents the long tradition of fishing in the region.

Yellowhead Highway → p. 64 leads via the cloud shrouded Skeena River to Hazelton, an important Tsimshian settlement centre. From here you can even make a short detour to Alaska, it is about a half day's drive on the Cassiar Highway to Stewart → p. 65, right on the border with the neighbouring country. The Yellowhead Highway stretches past secluded forests and lonely lakes with the odd farm or small town here and there. Along the way you will notice many dead pine trees – evidence of the spread of bark beetles. Only once you get close to the logging town of Prince George → p. 64 will you see large clear cuts where at least part of the dead wood is being utilised.

Highway 16 from Prince George connects you to the first route and travel to the Rockies. On the return journey to the south, take Highway 97 through the sunny ranch land of the Cariboo Region → p. 51. A must is the old gold rush town of Barkerville → p. 52, now a historic museum village. In Cache Creek the drive connects to the abovementioned route 1 and heads back via the Trans-Canada Highway to Vancouver.

The small town of Chemainus is famous for its outdoor gallery of large murals

## 4  WEST COAST TRAIL – SPECTACULAR PACIFIC WILDERNESS

Plan on about 6–8 days (in good weather conditions) to complete the most famous wilderness hike in Canada. The trail in the Pacific Rim National Park winds for 75km/47mi along the otherwise completely undeveloped coast, past deserted beaches and steep cliffs. You will have to hike during the summer because from October violent storms strike here. In the high season (July and August) a maximum of 50 hikers per day are allowed on the trail. Information and reservations see *www. pc.gc.ca/eng/pn-np/bc/pacificrim/activ/ activ6a.aspx*

In the 19th century storms on the west coast of Vancouver Island wrecked so many ships that the rocky coastline soon became known as the 'Graveyard of the Pacific'. In 1910 the government constructed a primitive rescue path for shipwreck survivors through the dense forest. This was the birth of the West Coast Trail, which since became Canada's most famous hiking trail.

To this day the path between Port Renfrew and Bamfield is still a challenge, even in good weather. Simple wooden bridges, cables and boarded walkways cross streams and enable climbs up the steep cliffs. At some places you can walk along the driftwood covered beaches but you often have to go back into the dense rainforests. If you do not mind getting wet, the sea lion colonies, waterfalls and wild coastlines more than compensate for all your discomfort.

The trail can be undertaken in both directions and you have to carry all your gear (rainwear!) and food with you. The park wardens keep the trail clear and there are primitive wilderness campsites. A bus shuttle *(www.trailbus.com)* provides a service for hikers and departs from Victoria → p. 47 and Nanaimo → p. 43 to the trail heads of the West Coast Trail and the southern neighbouring Juan de Fuca Trail.

# SPORTS & ACTIVITIES

Thanks to the pioneers, the outdoor life-style is a way of life for Canadians. So it is not surprising that even today every sport is enthusiastically enjoyed out in the fresh air. This is particularly true on the west coast, where smoking is frowned upon and fitness is the new religion.

It is also made easy for visitors as every major hotel and holiday resort has their own fitness centre as well as an activity desk, where you can book tee off times for the on-site golf course and obtain information about other activities. Several rental shops in parks and cities rent out canoes, bicycles and other sporting equipment – along with tips and maps. Organised day tours can also be booked at short notice. However, excursions that are several days long are best booked in advance.

## BIKING

Bicycles for day trips *(around C$20–35 per day, C$70–150 per week)* are readily available in the towns of the south. For longer rides, the Gulf Islands off Vancouver and the Okanagan Valley are ideal as are the old railway tracks in the Kettle Valley and the Rockies – here however, you do need to be quite fit. For f mountain bike enthusiasts there is the annual *Trans-Rockies Bike Race (www.transrockies.com)*.

Horseback riding, hiking, canoeing: the rugged Pacific coastline and the peaks of the Rockies offer an ideal destination for outdoor sports

### THE SKI STOP
In the summer of bike rental as well as single and multi-day tours in Banff National Park and on the Icefields Parkway. *203 A Bear St. Banff | tel. 403 7 60 16 50 | www. theskistop.com*

### WHISTLER MOUNTAIN BIKE PARK
The ultimate playground for mountain bikers: summer lifts and a 1200m/3900ft difference in altitude. *Whistler | tel. 866 2 18 96 90 | www.whistlerbike.com*

### CANOE, KAYAK & RUBBER DINGHY

The canoe was invented in Canada (they were originally made from birch bark, today from aluminium) and you can rent canoes in many lodges and from appro-

Alone with the vastness of nature – sea kayaking in Vancouver Island

priate suppliers. Sea kayaking tours, in the island labyrinth of the west coast, and rubber dinghy trips are also popular.

### CLEARWATER LAKE TOURS
Good canoe rental and also trips on the large, secluded lakes of the Wells Gray Provincial Park. *Clearwater | tel. 250 6 74 21 21 | www.clearwaterlaketours.com*

### ECO MARINE KAYAK CENTRE
Single and two seater kayak excursion around Vancouver, also for longer trips. *1668 Duranleau St. | Vancouver | tel. 604 6 89 75 75 | www.ecomarine.com*

### SUNWOLF
Full day rubber dinghy boat trips on the Elaho River near Whistler. For families, there are half day, gentler float trips. *70002 Squamish Valley Rd. | Brackendale | tel. 877 8 06 80 46 | www.sunwolf.net*

### INSIDER TIP ▶ TIMBERWOLF TOURS
Multi-day guided canoe trips and adventure tours in the Rockies. *Site 34, 51404 RR264 | Spruce Grove | Alberta | tel. 780 4 70 49 66 | www.timberwolftours.com*

## FISHING

Most anglers dream about landing a Pacific salmon but the fun is does not come cheap: from 500 dollars for two days and up to 5000 dollars for a week in an exclusive fishing resort. Amateur anglers may fish everywhere as long as they have a licence *(C$20–100 depending on the permit period)* and they are available in sporting goods stores and lodges.

### NAMUR LAKE LODGE
A remote fly-in lodge in northern Alberta with rustic log cabins. Sometimes it seems as if the huge northern pike and lake trout are just waiting to be caught. *Fort McMurray | tel. 780 7 91 92 99 | www. namurlakelodge.com*

### OAK BAY MARINE GROUP
The salmon angler's dreams can become a reality in the eight ships and fishing lodges of this resort group on Vancouver Island and the Queen Charlotte Islands. *1327 Beach Dr. | Victoria | tel. 800 6 63 70 90 | www.obmg.com*

## GOLF

Golf is a popular sport in Canada, and almost every little village has its own golf course. The greens are mostly open to the public so non-club members are welcome (also those without a handicap) and the green fees are affordable (C$40–80).

The most beautiful, but also the most expensive, courses are in the Rockies, such as the legendary Fairmont Course in Banff or Jasper National Park and those in Invermere or Kananaskis. These sites *www.albertagolf.org, www.golftherockies.net* and *www.britishcolumbiagolf.org* have more detailed information.

## HIKING

The largest selection of trails – signposted and well maintained – can be found in the national and provincial parks. The wardens in the respective visitor centres are more than happy to provide information about the best trails. Good networks are offered, for instance, in Banff, Yoho and Jasper national parks. Outside of the parks hiking is often difficult – in Canada wilderness really does mean wilderness. The *Trans Canada Trail*, which is currently being built, is the longest trail in the world running across all the provinces from the Pacific coast to Newfoundland. Some parts are already open for hiking *(info: www.tctrail.ca)*.

## HORSEBACK RIDING

Anyone can take part in a one or two hour trail ride. You need not be an experienced horse rider as they ride with the Western style saddles, and the horses walk very obediently in a row. Such rides can be booked at many ranches in the short term. However, for experienced riders there are also ranch holidays where you ride throughout the day with cowboys. Info: *www.bcguestranches.com* and *www.albertacountryvacation.com*.

### HOMEPLACE RANCH

Accommodation in a ranch, in the foothills of the Rockies, that is nearly a century old. *Site 2, RR 1 | Priddis. tel. 403 931 32 45 | www.homeplaceranch.com*

### INSIDER TIP ▶ TEN-EE-AH LODGE

Well maintained log cabin lodge with horseback riding program and other activities in British Columbia. There is also a campsite. *Lac La Hache | tel. 250 4 34 97 45 | www.ten-ee-ah.bc.ca*

## ROPE COURSES & ZIP LINES

Adrenaline rush: in recent years rope and adventure courses for adults (and children) have been popping up throughout Canada. Zip lining through canyons and over streams or above the forest has become a popular activity. All the guides are trained and the equipment is safe and well secured – guaranteed fun. For an overview: *www.ziplinerider.com* and *www.wildplay.com*

## WINTER SPORTS

The powder snow in the Rockies is legendary. Ski areas such as Banff, Lake Louise, Fernie, or Big White offer excellent ski slopes. The largest area is Whistler on the west coast. Experienced skiers can also enjoy the thrill of heli-skiing in central British Columbia.

### CANADIAN MOUNTAIN HOLIDAYS

Heli-skiing trips into the remote mountains on the western edge of the Rockies. *Banff | tel. 403 7 62 71 00 | www.canadianmountainholidays.com*

# TRAVEL WITH KIDS

Canada is also a very child-friendly country. The Canadians themselves travel with their offspring during the holiday months of July and August and the tourist infrastructure is geared for families. In the restaurants there are special children's menus and child seats. Most hotels offer children's beds and cots – sometimes at no additional cost – and many motels have paddling pools for the little ones next to the main swimming pool.

All activities on the sea and the lakes are fun. Canoeing, for instance, is a lot of fun and there are lakes are around every corner. Ghost towns and trapper forts are there to be explored and many places have their own children's museum. Travelling in a mobile home is also very popular: the vehicle creates a familiar, consistent environment while the outdoors and camping offer real adventure, making their holiday in Canada a success.

## VANCOUVER

INSIDER TIP **GRANVILLE ISLAND KIDS MARKET** (U B5–6) (*m b5–6*)
A whole warehouse full of toys, fun crayons, colourful sweets and other temptations. Just across the road is a large model train museum. *Daily 10am–6pm | Granville Island | www.kidsmarket.ca*

Holidays in Canada are great for children – spotting bears and eagles by day, toasting marshmallows around the campfire by night

### MINIATURE TRAINS, A WATER PARK AND SECOND BEACH POOL
(U C1, A2) (*𝄞 c1, a2*)

There are a variety of activities for children in the large city park in summer: the water park at *Lumberman's Arch (families C$3.50/ per person)* has spray fountains and water cannons, a narrow gauge railway makes its rounds, and at *Second Beach (families C$3/per person)* there is a large heated outdoor pool with water slide and children's area. *Stanley Park*

### SCIENCE WORLD (U E–F5) (*𝄞 e–f5*)

The Expo 86 sphere is now a children's technology museum with interactive experiments and a surround screen cinema. *Mon–Fri 10am–5pm, Sat/Sun 10am–6pm | admission C$23.50, children C$16.75 | 1455 Quebec St. | www.scienceworld.ca*

## VANCOUVER ISLAND

INSIDER TIP HORNE LAKE CAVES
PROV. PARK (133 D5) (*D14*)
Headlamps light the way into the park's mysterious caves and there is quite a lot to see including fossils, crystal formations, waterfalls and stalactites and stalagmites. *Guided tour C$24, children 5 years and older C$20, also longer tours. Phone reservation: tel. 250 2 48 78 29 | www.hornelake. com | 25km/15mi north-west of Parksville*

### MCLEAN MILL (133 D5) (*D14*)
Take a steam train through the forest to an old steam-powered sawmill in. There, you will be briefed like a new worker 100 years ago. *Daily 10.30am–5.15pm, Thu–Sun journey by steam train and steam operation of the sawmill | admission C$10, children C$6.25, steam train C$30, children C$18.75 | E & N train station | 3100 Kingsway | Port Alberni*

Dressed and ready for the powpow

### MINIATURE WORLD (133 D6) (*E15*)
A museum full of dollhouses and miniature scenes from fairy-tales and children's books, in the Empress Hotel. *Daily in summer 9am–9pm otherwise 9am–5pm | admission C$12, children C$8 | 649 Humboldt St. Victoria*

### QUINSAM RIVER HATCHERY
(133 D5) (*D14*)
Millions of juvenile salmon are held in large ponds and rearing channels before being released so that they can then return here to spawn. Returning adult salmon are captured and held in holding ponds. *5km/3mi north-west of Campbell River. Daily 8am–4pm | admission free | 4217 Argonaut Rd.*

## BRITISH COLUMBIA

### KOOTENAY RIVER RUNNERS
(134 C5) (*H15*)
Adventurous rafting on the Kicking Horse and the Kootenay rivers and canoe trips on the Columbia (children over 5 years of age), also picnics. *From C$49, children from C$39 | Hwy. 93 | Radium Hot Springs | tel. 250 3 47 92 10 | www.raftingtherockies.com*

### PENTICTON CHANNEL (133 F5) (*F14*)
Floating down the channel between the two lakes in Penticton on an inner tube is a lot of fun. *Coyote Cruises (tel. 250 4 92 2115) rent out tubes (approx. C$10) and organise transport back. Hwy. 97 at the northern end of the channel*

### ZIPTREK ECOTOURS ☺
(133 D–E7) (*E14*)
One of the oldest and most experienced zip line companies in the world, children from 6 years are taken along in tandem rides. The platforms and zip lines are designed in such a way that they do not impact on the forest nature. *Whistler | tel. 866 9 35 00 01 | www.ziptrek.com*

# TRAVEL WITH KIDS

## ROCKY MOUNTAINS

**LUXTON MUSEUM** (134 C5) (*H13*)
The Native American museum is also interesting for smaller children as there are activities such as feather jewellery craft and how to construct a tepee. *Daily in the summer 11am–6pm, otherwise 1pm–5pm | admission C$10, children C$ 2.50 | 1 Birch Ave. | Banff*

## ALBERTA

**ALBERTA BIRDS OF PREY CENTRE** (135 D6) (*J14*)
A sanctuary for birds of prey where injured hawks, owls and eagles are nursed back to health. Flying demonstration every 90 minutes. *Daily in summer 9.30am–5pm | admission C$9.50, children C$6.50 | Coaldale/Lethbridge | www.burrowingowl.com*

**CALGARY ZOO & PREHISTORIC PARK** (135 D5) (*H14*)
A zoo with Siberian tigers and the indigenous animals of Canada. The main attraction is the 'Jurassic Park' with 20 life-sized dinosaurs. *Daily 9am–5pm | admission C$21, children C$13 | 1300 Zoo Rd. NE | Calgary | www.calgaryz oo.org*

**RAFTER SIX RANCH** (134 C5) (*H13*)
Good for a family day out: riding on horses and ponies, horse-drawn carriage rides and rafting tours in a beautiful setting. *Seebe | tel. 403 6 73 36 22 | www.raftersix.com*

**ROYAL TYRRELL MUSEUM OF PALAEONTOLOGY** (135 D4) (*J13*)
Care to dig for dinosaur fossils? The palaeontology museum offers excavations for different age groups, under the guidance of scientists. There are also INSIDER TIP special guided tours for children *(admission C$11, children C$6, daily programmes from C$28 | 1500 N Dinosaur Trail | Drumheller | tel. 403 8 23 77 07 | www.tyrrellmuseum.com*

Large head, sharp teeth: a fierce Albertosaurus in the Royal Tyrrell Museum

**WEST EDMONTON MALL/GALAXYLAND AMUSEMENT PARK** (135 D3) (*J12*)
The world's largest indoor amusement park with roller coaster rides, carousels and a 3D cinema. Numerous other attractions for children: large wave pool with slides, ice skating rink, climbing course, mini golf and shows with sea lions. *Daily in the summer from 10am | day ticket for children C$26, also single rides | 87th Ave./170th St. | Edmonton | www.Wem.ca*

## NORTHERN CANADA

**WILD PLAY YUKON** (128 C2) (*B6*)
Adventure recreation area with zip lines and climbing ladders, nets and ropes for children from 7 years who would like to tackle the challenges here with (or without) their parents. *Adults C$43, children C$23, zip lining C$100 | Mount Sima, Whitehorse. tel. 867 6 68 45 57 | www.wildplay.com*

# FESTIVALS & EVENTS

In summer, every cultural group, every village celebrates their own events alongside the major festivals: pioneer days, lumberjack competitions, rodeos and Native American powwows, but there are also folk and music festivals. It is best to visit the local visitor's centre to find out what is being celebrated where.

## OFFICIAL HOLIDAYS

**1 Jan** *New Year's Day*; **Good Friday; Easter Monday; Monday before the 25th of May** *Victoria Day*; **1 July** *Canada Day* (national holiday); **1st Monday in Aug** *provincial holiday* in British Columbia and Alberta; **1st Monday in Sept** *Labour Day*; **2nd Monday in Oct** *Thanksgiving*; **11 Nov** *Remembrance Day*; **25/26 Dec** *Christmas*

## FESTIVALS

### FEBRUARY
Whitehorse: ▶ *Sourdough Rendezvous* with ▶ *Frostbite Music Festival:* 3 days of music for the start and end of the famous dog sled race the ▶ *Yukon Quest*

### MAY
Vancouver: cowboy fans can experience a real rodeo in the suburb of Cloverdale. *www.cloverdalerodeo.com*
Victoria: on ▶ *Victoria Day* colourful parades, concerts, and races and the following weekend is the traditional regatta ▶ *Swiftsure Race*

### JUNE
Vancouver: the Chinese ▶ *Dragon Boat Festival* is in mid June; then the famous ▶ *Vancouver International Jazz Festival*, *www.coastaljazz.ca*
High River: ▶ *Chuckwagon races:* pioneer wagon races in mid June

### JULY
▶ *Canada Day:* 1 July, Canada's national day is celebrated with picnics, parades and street parties. Williams Lake marks the day with a ▶ *Rodeo,* Dawson City with a gold panning competion and the ▶ *River Quest Canoe Race*
Calgary: in early July cowboys come from all over the world to compete in the world's largest rodeo, the ▶ ★ *Calgary Stampede*. *www.calgarystampede.com*

Rodeos and axe contests: in summer the long weekends are especially popular for festivals and events

Nanaimo: ▶ *Marine Festival and Bathtub Race:* at the end of July over 100 state-of-the-art bathtub boats make their way to Vancouver. *www.bathtubbing.com*

Yellowknife: ▶ *Folk on the Rocks:* 24 hours of music under the midnight sun, mid July. *folkontherocks.com*

Medicine Hat: ▶ INSIDER TIP *Exhibition & Stampede:* car racing, rodeo, farmers' market and parades (last weekend of July). *www.mhstampede.com*

### JUNE–AUGUST

From July until late August young artists from all regions meet for the ▶ *Banff Arts Festival* with concerts, theatre, and ballet

### AUGUST

Squamish: ▶ ★ *Squamish Days Loggers Sports:* lumberjacks display their skill and stamina on the first weekend in August. *squamishdays.ca.*

Vancouver Island: lumberjacks compete with their axes at the Campbell River ▶ ● *Salmon Festival*

Lethbridge: ▶ *Whoop–Up Days:* middle of the month there is the famous folk festival and rodeo

Abbotsford: ▶ *International Air show* with historical aircraft (middle of the month)

Dawson City: ▶ ★ *Discovery Days:* on the 17th Aug. the town celebrates the discovery of gold in the Yukon

Vancouver: ▶ *Pacific National Exhibition:* agricultural show and fair with concerts and rides. *www.PNE.ca*

### SEPTEMBER

Dawson City: on the first weekend participants in the ▶ INSIDER TIP *Klondike International Outhouse Race* run through the town with decorated toilets on wheels

Kelowna: the wineries of the Okanagan Valley host the ▶ *Fall Wine Festival*

# LINKS, BLOGS, APPS & MORE

LINKS

▶ www.Canada.travel A comprehensive site that includes places to go, things to do, trip ideas and videos. Also recommendations by specially trained travel agents with experience of Canada

▶ www.parkscanada.ca Great website with detailed descriptions of the individual national parks. The site includes videos, 3D representations and features such as an interactive map where you select your region for specials and highlights

▶ www.weatheroffice.gc.ca Official Canadian weather service with satellite imagery, rain radar – and surprisingly accurate weather forecasts for even the smallest town in this massive country

▶ www.aboriginalbc.com Site promoting cultural tourism with Native American offerings including lodges, canoe trips and cultural centres

▶ maps.Google.com Everybody knows Google Maps, but the street view mode for Whistler and the Rockies also shows the ski slopes!

▶ www.travel.bc.ca An excellent resource for accommodation, activities and tours and there are also great discount deals and featured listings

APPS

▶ Visit Vancouver A tour through the city, interactive dining options, upcoming and current events, photos and videos for iPad

▶ Live Nation Information and ticket centre for concert tours, clubs and venues in Vancouver or Calgary. Details at www.livenation.com

▶ OpenTable A useful app for restaurant reservations, with a good selection (especially in the cities) of restaurants and you can also use it to find restaurants closest to your current location and see what tables are available, last minute reservations are often an option

Regardless of whether you are still preparing your trip or already in Canada: these addresses will provide you with more information, videos and networks to make your holiday even more enjoyable

BLOGS & FORUMS

▶ www.straight.com/blogra The comprehensive online blog of Vancouver's Georgia Straight newspaper. Numerous features and articles about the city's nightlife, art, and restaurants scene

▶ ibackpackcanada.com An informative and entertaining independent travel guide written by Corbin Fraser who decided to backpack from coast to coast for six months three years ago and hasn't stopped since. The ideal travel blog for those interested in travelling through Canada on a budget.

▶ www.Whistler.com/blog News from the sports scene in Whistler with events, cool locations etc.

▶ music.cbc.ca/#/radio3/blogs All about the Canada music scene, indie bands and mainstream, right up to date and with tips about upcoming concerts, and podcasts

VIDEOS & STREAMS

▶ www.cbc.ca/north Winter in the Arctic? Or summer? Short films, photos and news articles of the regional broadcaster portray life in the Yukon and the Northwest Territories

▶ www.yukonquest.com Everything you need to know about the world's hardest and longest sled dog race; with videos and live tracking

▶ www.MuchMusic.com Music videos and interviews with Canadian pop and rock stars from the most important music station in the country

▶ www.5min.com Extensive video selection with numerous short films about Canada – search under travel and select the respective province or city name

NETWORK

▶ www.airbnb.com An online booking site for guesthouses and private accommodation with lots of listings for western Canada.

▶ www.9flats.com A little more expensive, this site lists private accommodation (search under the town where you would like to stay over). There are listings for houses, apartments and rooms (even an igloo)

# TRAVEL TIPS

## ARRIVAL

*Air Canada* and most national carriers have regular direct flights to Vancouver or to Calgary with domestic flight connections to all the major cities. There are also numerous independent regional and local airlines that focus on the more remote regions and charter airlines that offer seasonal specials. In the peak tourist season (July and Aug) flights are often fully booked so you should book as early as possible – several months in advance – this also applies for the trans-Atlantic route, for motor homes and the longer ferry passages.

The major car rental companies like *Avis*, *Hertz* and *National/Alamo* have representatives at all the airports. Taxis and airport buses are also available to take you into the city centre. If you have booked a motor home, the rental company will usually collect you at the airport. An even better option is for you to first go into the city and then collect the vehicle the next morning – well-rested for your first trip with the unfamiliar vehicle.

## BUS & TRAIN

*Greyhound* and several regional bus lines (e.g. Brewster, Red Arrow Express) connect all the larger towns. Information (also about express buses and student fares) in travel agencies or at www.greyhound.ca.
Another wonderful way to see Canada is to travel from coast to coast on the legendary Trans-Canada route from Vancouver to Montréaland there is also the *Rocky Mountaineer* from Vancouver to Calgary or vice versa (book several months in advance, www.rockymountaineer.com). The rail company VIA Rail *(www.viarail.ca)* offers a *Canrailpass* for their entire network.

## CAMPING & YOUTH HOSTELS

Canada's public camping sites are beautiful, they are usually situated next to the water in national parks and they all have a fireplace, wooden benches, water pump and a simple outhouse and cost C$10–30 per night. Private, luxuriously equipped sites can be found on the outskirts of cities and outside the national parks (prices approx. C$15–45). Camping rough is not prohibited (except in the parks), but is frowned upon in the populated areas. Camping spaces in national parks can be booked beforehand at www.pccamping.ca, other parks in BC, www.discovercamping.ca.
The accommodation by the *Canadian Hostelling Association (www.hihostels.ca)*

## RESPONSIBLE TRAVEL

It doesn't take a lot to be environmentally friendly whilst travelling. Don't just think about your carbon footprint whilst flying to and from your holiday destination but also about how you can protect nature and culture abroad. As a tourist it is especially important to respect nature, look out for local products, cycle instead of driving, save water and much more. If you would like to find out more about eco-tourism please visit: www.ecotourism.org

Holiday from start to finish: the most important addresses and information for your trip to western Canada

costs from C$15 per night, some also have single and double rooms available from C$40. In the large cities backpackers can stay at the YMCA (for men) and the YWCA (for women), in the countryside you will often find small home hostels.

## CAR HIRE

The minimum age to rent a car is 21, often 25 years. Your national driving licence will suffice. You should book cars or camper vans through a travel agent several months in advance, this is usually cheaper and safer. One way routes often mean penalties.

## CONSULATES & EMBASSIES

**US EMBASSY IN VANCOUVER**
*1095 W Pender Street | Vancouver | BC V6E 2M6 | tel. +1 604 6 85 43 11 | canada.us embassy.gov*

**BRITISH CONSULATE IN VANCOUVER**
*Suite 800, 1111 Melville Street | Vancouver | BC V6E 3V6 | tel. +1 604 6 83 4421 | british consulate.vancouver@fco.gov.uk*

**AUSTRALIAN CONSULATE IN VANCOUVER**
*Suite 2050-1075 | West Georgia Street | Vancouver | BC V6E 3C9 | tel. +1 604 6 84 1177 | www.canada.embassy.gov.au*

## CUSTOMS

The following goods can be imported duty free into Canada: 1.1 litres of spirits, 200 cigarettes, 50 cigars or 250g tobacco, 50g perfume or 250g eau de toilette and gifts up to a value of C$60. Plants and food-

# BUDGETING

| Coffee | £1.20–£2.40/US$2–$4 |
| --- | --- |
| | *for a pot of coffee* |
| Beer | £3.30–£5/US$5.20–$8 |
| | *for a beer in a restaurant* |
| Salmon | £12–£20/US$20–$33 |
| | *for a piece with side dish* |
| Boots | £33–£57/US$52–$90 |
| | *for original cowboy boots* |
| Tour | £40–£65/US$65–$100 |
| | *for a half day raft or bicycle trip* |
| Petrol | £0.90/US$1.35 |
| | *for a litre unleaded* |

stuffs (especially fresh food) may not be imported.

## DOMESTIC FLIGHTS & FERRIES

Air Canada and some regional airlines offer fares discounted by 40 per cent for routes within Canada. But you should buy these tickets before your trip. Otherwise, flights on regional airlines such as Air North and West Jet are often cheaper when purchased online.

Ferries travel hourly between Vancouver Island and the mainland and do not require advance booking. However, you will need to book early for the 15 hour trip between Port Hardy and Prince Rupert through the Inside Passage and for the equally impressive Discovery Coast Passage to Bella Coola (in a travel agency).

For further information once you are in Canada: *tel. 250 3 86 34 31 or 1 88 82 23 37 79 | www.bcferries.com*

## DRIVING

You can drive with your national driver's license for up to three months (Yukon: 1 month). In all provinces it is compulsory to wear seat elts and it is best to refrain from drinking and driving. On the major roads the maximum speed is 80km/50mi or 100km/60mi, in towns 50km/30mi and on motorways 110km/65mi.

Traffic regulations are standard but there are certain unusual features: at the traffic light you can also turn right on red, on multi-lane roads you may overtake but school buses with their hazard lights on may never be passed, not even from the opposite side. The Canadian Automobile Club (CAA) also helps members of foreign clubs (identity required; emergency number: *tel. 800 2 22 43 57*).

## ELECTRICITY

Current is 110 volts, 60Ht. Appliances such as shavers and hair dryers from other countries will need a transformer and you will also need a plug adaptor for Canada's two-pin sockets.

# BOOKS & FILMS

▶ **The Tenderness of Wolves** – Set in the Northern Territory in the 1860s, this novel by Stef Penney won the 2006 Costa Book of the Year award. The story revolves around the brutal murder of a Hudson's Bay Company trapper and the events that follow his death (2006)

▶ **Empire of the Bay: The Company of Adventurers that Seized a Continent** – Peter C Newman's excellently written book is full of interesting facts; it details the impact of Hudson's Bay Company and the fur trade's role in the formation of Canada (2000)

▶ **Generation X: Tales for an Accelerated Culture** – Douglas Coupland's 1991 cult novel about a group of youths in an affluent society popularised the term 'Generation X' and 'McJob'. Coupland lives in Vancouver

▶ **Overexposed: A Granville Island Mystery** – Set in and around Vancouver Michael Blair's mystery novel follows photographer Tom McCall who wakes to a crashing hangover, lingerie in his dishwasher and a dead man on the deck of his floating home. Fast paced and complex plot (2006)

▶ **Three Day Road** – Joseph Boyden's novel tells the story of Xavier, a young Cree Indian, who returns from the First World War and recovers through the stories of his aunt Niska (2006)

▶ **Atanarjuat: The Fast Runner** – The film poetically and grippingly tells the story of an Inuit myth. It was the first Canadian film to be written, directed and acted in Inuktitut (2001)

▶ **Brokeback Mountain** – Shot almost entirely in the picturesque Canadian Rockies in southern Alberta, the epic romantic drama, directed by Ang Lee (2005) and starring Heath Ledger and Jake Gyllenhaal, is based on a short story by Canadian author E. Annie Proulx

## EMERGENCY SERVICES

*Dial 911* or *0* for the operator

## HEALTH

Medical care in Canada is very good – but expensive. A day in the hospital can cost C$1000 or more. Ensure that you have foreign health insurance. Medicine can be bought in a pharmacy or drugstore. One concern in summer for campers and hikers are mosquitoes. Load up with insect repellents and sprays and wear trousers and long sleeved shirts when hiking.

Banff Alberta National Park borders the time zone boundary

## IMMIGRATION

Tourists from the USA, EU countries and most Commonwealth countries (UK, Australia and New Zealand) only need a valid passport to enter Canada – passport holders from other countries must apply for visas. Passports issued after October 2006 must contain a data chip and even if small children are registered in the passport of the parents, they will need their own passport. The immigration officer at your point of arrival decides your length of stay – generally not longer than six months. If you decide to extend your stay once you have arrived in Canada, you will need to apply for an extension at the nearest Canada Immigration Centre. You will need to do this well in advance of the expiry of your current authorised date. If you plan to cross the border into the US first check to see if you qualify to enter under the Visa Waiver Program (VWP) which allows you to travel to the US for 90 days or less without having to obtain a visa.

## INFORMATION

The Canadian Tourist Office website *www. canada.travel* provides extensive informa-tion about Canada's attractions and ac-tivities. There are also competitions and travel ideas. There are links to the indi-vidual provinces, such as Alberta and British Columbia and you can also request brochures and maps for each region. In Canada itself you will find well signposted *Info Centres* and *Visitors Bureaus*.
Alberta: *www.travelalberta.co*
British Columbia: *www.britishcolumbia. travel* and *www.hellobv.com*
Yukon: *www.travelyukon.co*.

## INTERNET & WI-FI

Canada has an excellent network and hotels offer high speed Internet access for about C$10–15 a day. **INSIDER TIP** You can check you mail and surf the web free of charge or for a small fee in all the public libraries in Canada. With your own laptop or smart phone you find Wi-Fi (free or with a password from the staff) in many hotels, coffee shops and public places.

## MONEY & CREDIT CARDS

Local currency is the Canadian dollar (= 100 cents). Bank notes are available in 5,

# CURRENCY CONVERTER

| £ | C$ | C$ | £ |
|---|-----|-----|------|
| 1 | 1.60 | 1 | 0.6 |
| 3 | 4.80 | 3 | 1.90 |
| 5 | 8 | 5 | 3.10 |
| 13 | 20.80 | 13 | 8.10 |
| 40 | 64 | 40 | 25 |
| 75 | 120 | 75 | 47 |
| 120 | 192 | 120 | 75 |
| 250 | 400 | 250 | 156 |
| 500 | 800 | 500 | 312.50 |

At the time of going to press, US$1 ≈ C$1.
For current exchange rates see www.xe.com

10, 20, 50 and 100 dollars and coins in ¢1 (penny), ¢5 (nickel), ¢10 (dime), ¢25 (quarter), C$1 (loonie) and C$2 (toonie). Banks are usually open from 10am to 3pm. They cash traveller's cheques (made out in Canadian or US dollars), but do not exchange any other currency. You can exchange foreign currencies into dollars at airports and major hotels (but the rate may be bad). Divide your holiday fund into various payment methods: approx. C$100 cash for the arrival, a credit card for the majority of daily expenses (Visa or Mastercard is accepted everywhere at petrol stations, restaurants, etc.), as well as a debit cards which you can use to draw cash from most ATMs at a favourable exchange rate. To be extra safe you can also take a few hundred dollars in traveller's cheques (they are accepted in shops and restaurants and you get your change in cash).

## OPENING HOURS

Shops are usually open Mon–Sat from 9.30am–6pm, large shopping malls, 10am–9pm and Sun noon–5pm. Supermarkets are often open evenings and weekends, in the large cities some are open around the clock. Many museums are closed on Mondays.

## PHONE & MOBILE PHONE

All the telephone numbers in Canada have seven digits, moreover, a 3–digit prefix for long distance and within some cities (area code). When dialling any number (local or long distance) you must include the area code. The operator (dial 0) will help you with any telephone problems and also sets up collect calls. Toll free numbers for hotels or tour booking begin with the prefix *800*, *866*, *877* or *888* Code for Germany: *+1149*. After Austria: *+1143*. In Switzerland: *+1141*. Then choose the area code without the first zero and then the number. Code for Canada: *+1*. European tri or quad band phones also function in Canada but usually in the cities and in the south of the provinces. Calls from phone booths of using a prepaid phone card are cheaper than using your mobile. The cards are available at petrol stations and grocery stores. For a longer stay it is worth getting a Canadian SIM card and using it with your (unlocked!) mobile.

## POST

Post offices are open Mon–Fri 9am–6pm and Sat 8am–noon. Postage for an airmail letter or postcard to the US costs C$1.05 and C$1.80 for international mail (up to 30g).

## TAX

Canada has a 5% Goods and Services Tax *(GST)* levied by the federal government and then each province has their own Provincial Sales Tax *(PST)*. British Columbia has a PST of 7%. Some taxes are only added to the purchase price at the cash register.

20% of the invoice amount. Hotel porters get about C$1–2 per piece of luggage.

## TIME

Canada has multiple time zones. In British Columbia and in the Yukon it is Pacific Time (PDT) which is eight hours behind Coordinated Universal (UTC), in the North-west Territories and Alberta it is Mountain Time (MDT) which is six hours behind Coordinated Universal (UTC).

## TIPPING

A service charge is not included in the restaurants and the standard tip is 15–

## WEATHER, WHEN TO GO

Apart from the coastal regions of British Columbia, western Canada has an extreme climate which ensures cold, snowy winters and dry, hot summers. The best time to travel (and high season) is mid June to late August. May and September however are also just as nice – with sunny days and cool nights. And in the autumn the vibrant colours of the forest foliage make a very beautiful display. February and March are best for snowmobiling and skiing in the Rockies.

# WEATHER IN VANCOUVER

| | Jan | Feb | March | April | May | June | July | Aug | Sept | Oct | Nov | Dec |
|---|---|---|---|---|---|---|---|---|---|---|---|---|
| Daytime temperatures in °C/°F | 6/43 | 8/46 | 11/52 | 14/57 | 18/64 | 21/70 | 23/73 | 23/73 | 19/66 | 14/57 | 9/48 | 7/45 |
| Nighttime temperatures in °C/°F | 1/34 | 1/34 | 3/37 | 5/41 | 8/46 | 11/52 | 13/55 | 12/54 | 10/50 | 7/45 | 4/39 | 2/36 |
| Sunshine hours/day | 2 | 3 | 4 | 6 | 7 | 7 | 9 | 8 | 6 | 4 | 2 | 1 |
| Precipitation days/month | 17 | 13 | 14 | 11 | 7 | 5 | 4 | 7 | 7 | 15 | 16 | 18 |
| Water temperatures in °C/°F | 8/46 | 7/45 | 8/46 | 9/48 | 11/52 | 13/57 | 14/57 | 14/57 | 13/55 | 12/54 | 11/52 | 10/50 |

# NOTES

# ROAD ATLAS

The green line ▬▬ indicates the Trips & Tours (p. 98–103)
The blue line ▬▬ indicates The perfect route (p. 30–31)

All tours are also marked on the pull-out map

Photo: Dawson Creek, Alaska Highway

ENTERING THE
FAMOUS
HIGHWAY
...REEK B.C.

ALBERTA
POOL
ELEVATORS LTD
DAWSON CREEK

ALBERTA
POOL
ELEVATORS LTD
DAWSON CREEK

ART GALLERY

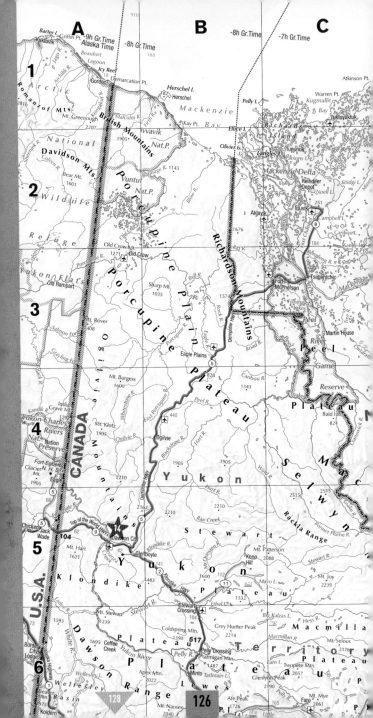

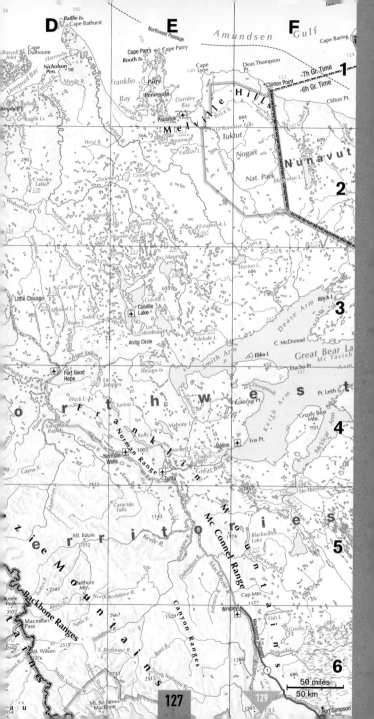

**D**

**E**

**F**

Baillie Is. Cape Bathurst
192
26
Russell Inlet
Cape Dalhousie
Harrowby
Nicholson Pen. 98
Liverpool Bay
Campbell I.
Anderson R.
Mason R.
Wood R.
Kaglik La.

*Amundsen Gulf*

Cape Baring
Cape Baring
Island

Northwest Passage
Cape Parry Cape Parry
Booth Is.
Franklin Bay
Parry Peninsula
Langton Bay
Darnley Bay
140 Cape Lyon
Deas Thompson Pt.
123 Clinton Point
-7h Gr. Time
-6h Gr. Time
124

**1**

Horton R.
Paulatuk
Brock R.
La Ronciare Falls
Clifton Pt.
147

**Melville Hills**
366
Binamey
Fallaize L.
Tuktut
884
Rorella
609

West R.
290

Crossley Lakes
138

Wolverine R.
230

Andrew R.
Simpson R.

Tadenet L.

Grandi L.
Townsend

Navelin R.
333
245

Nogait Nat. Park

**Nunavut**

Bluenose L.
442
Mts. R.

**2**

Little Chicago
385

Manuel L.
280

Carcajou R.
Tadek L.
Roney L.
Bluefish R.
Hare Indian R.

Tedit L.
Aubry L.

Lac Maunoir
280

Colville Lake
655
Colville L.

Lac desBoisi
326
Kilekale L.
210

Horton L.
686
166

152

Dease Arm
Ritch I.

**3**

Arctic Circle

Fort Good Hope
291

Chick L.
Humer R.
Sans Sault Rapids
Carcajou R.

Turton L.

Lac Jacques

Tunago Lo
262

Smith Arm
652
Ekka I.
C. McDonnel

Great Bear La
Mc Tavish

Etacho Pt.
137

**4**

**orth** **w** **est**
Kokeragi Pt.
Deeppass R.
Pt. Leith

Mahony L.
Brackett L.
Kelly L.
Minisicol R.
St. Charles Rapids
Déline
Fox Pt.

Grizzly Bear Mtn.
701

Kelith Arm
McVicar Arm

Norman Range
Norman Wells
Tulita
Great Bear R.
3132

Gayna R.
10

**orth** **Franklin** **Mountains**

Mountain R.
Caracuja Falls

Mt. Eduni
2352
Keele R.
1003
1143 407

Redstone R.
Dahadinni R.
Mackenzie R.
Markhogzee

Blackwater Lake
Blackwater R.
Keller L.
217

**5**

**ziee Mountains**
**erritories**

Keele Peak
2972
Tawu R.
2383
Delthore Mtn.
North Redstone R.
2667
Natla R.

Redstone R.
2713
S. Redstone R.
2515

**Mc Connel Range**
**Canyon Ranges**

Redstone R.
Root R.
North Nahanni R.

Cap Mtn.
1577
Wrigley

1266

Fish L.
Greasy L.
Bulmer L.

Hollow L.
686

**6**

**Backbone Ranges**
Macmillan Pass
Mt. Wilson
2515
276
South Nahanni R.

Mt. Sir James MacBrien

Cli L.
1295
Fort Simpson

127 129

50 miles
50 km

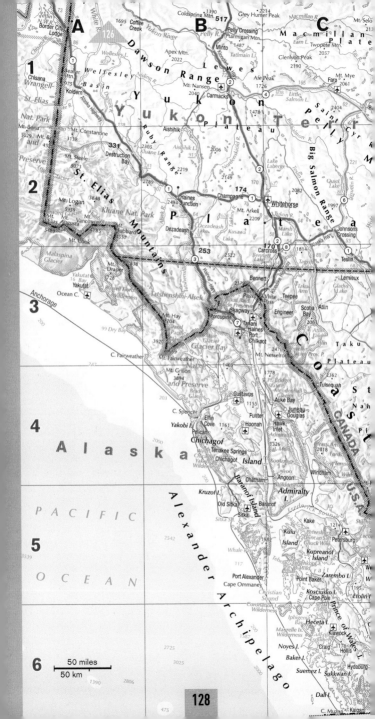

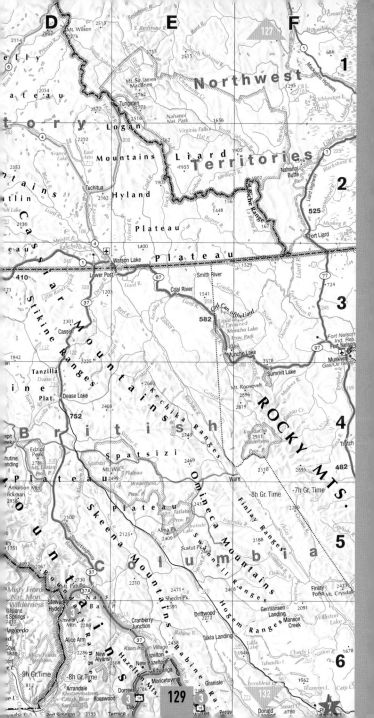

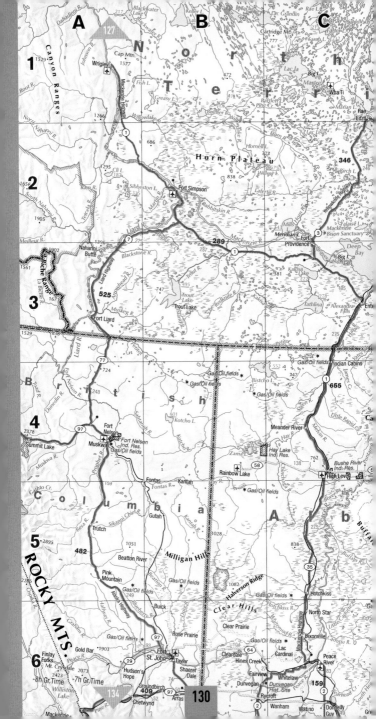

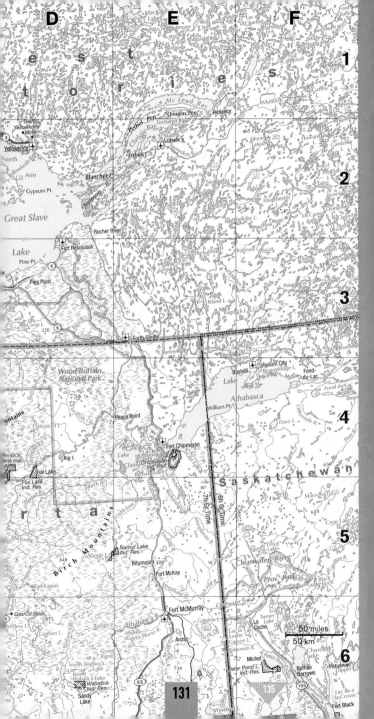

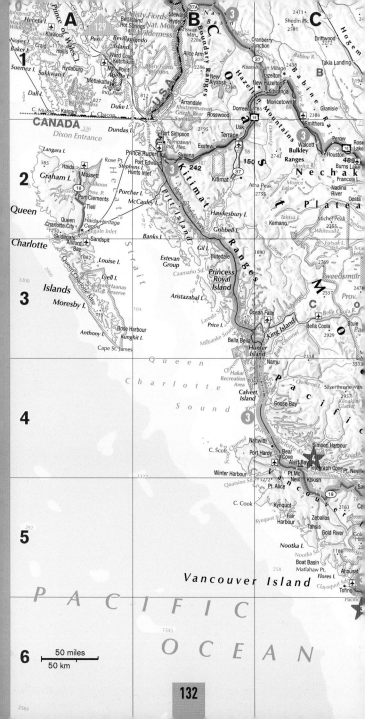

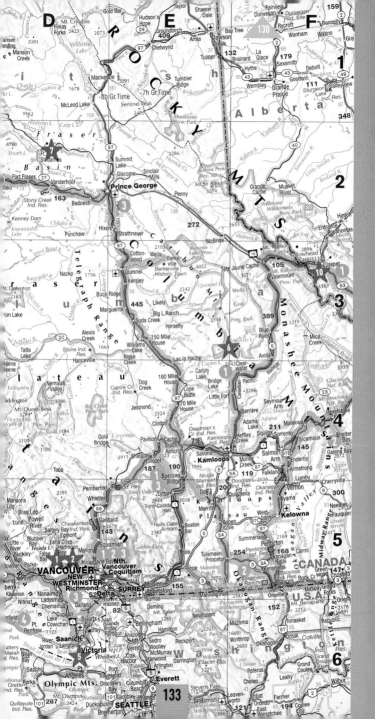

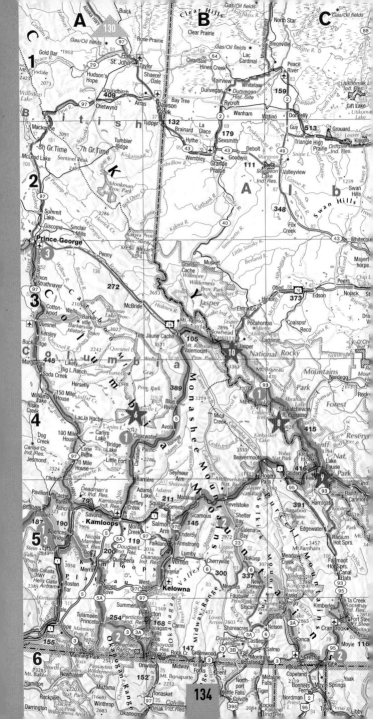

# KEY TO ROAD ATLAS

| | | |
|---|---|---|
| Highway, multilane divided road<br>- under construction<br>Autobahn, mehrspurige Straße - in Bau |  | Autoroute, route à plusieurs voies<br>- en construction   Autopista, carretera<br>de más carriles - en construcción |
| Trunk road - under construction<br>Fernverkehrsstraße - in Bau |  | Route à grande circulation - en construction<br>Ruta de larga distancia - en construcción |
| Principal highway<br>Hauptstraße | | Route principale<br>Carretera principal |
| Secondary road<br>Nebenstraße | | Route secondaire<br>Carretera secundaria |
| Practicable road, track<br>Fahrweg, Piste | | Chemin carrossable, piste<br>Camino vecinal, pista |
| Road numbering<br>Straßennummerierung |  | Numérotage des routes<br>Numeración de carreteras |
| Distances in mi. (USA), in km (CDN)<br>Entfernungen in mi. (USA), in km (CDN) |  | Distances en mi. (USA), en km (CDN)<br>Distancias en mi. (USA), en km (CDN) |
| Height in metres - Pass<br>Höhe in Meter - Pass | | Altitude en mètres - Col<br>Altura en metros - Puerto de montaña |
| Railway<br>Eisenbahn | | Chemin-de-fer<br>Ferrocarril |
| Car ferry - Shipping route<br>Autofähre - Schifffahrtslinie | | Bac autos - Ligne maritime<br>Transportador de automóviles - Ferrocarriles |
| Major international airport - Airport<br>Wichtiger internationaler Flughafen - Flughafen | ✈ ✈ | Aéroport important international - Aéroport<br>Aeropuerto importante internacional - Aeropuerto |
| International boundary - provincial boundary<br>Internationale Grenze - Provinzgrenze | | Frontière nationale - Frontière provinciale<br>Frontera nacional - Frontera provincial |
| Undefined boundary<br>Unbestimmte Grenze | | Frontière d'État non définie<br>Frontera indeterminada |
| Time zone boundary<br>Zeitzonengrenze | -4h Greenwich Time<br>-3h Greenwich Time | Limite de fuseau horaire<br>Límite del huso horario |
| National capital<br>Hauptstadt eines souveränen Staates | **OTTAWA** | Capitale nationale<br>Capital de un estado soberano |
| Provincial capital<br>Hauptstadt einer Provinz | **TORONTO** | Capitale d'un chef-lieu<br>Capital de provincia |
| Restricted area<br>Sperrgebiet | | Zone interdite<br>Zona prohibida |
| Indian reservation - National park<br>Indianerreservat - Nationalpark | | Réserve d'indiens - Parc national<br>Reserva de indios - Parque nacional |
| Interesting cultural monument<br>Sehenswertes Kulturdenkmal | ★ *Disneyland* | Monument culturel intéressant<br>Monumento cultural de interés |
| Interesting natural monument<br>Sehenswertes Naturdenkmal | ★ *Niagara Falls* | Monument naturel intéressant<br>Monumento natural de interés |
| Well, Salt lake<br>Brunnen, Salzsee | ⌣ 🌐 | Puits, Lac salé<br>Pozo, Lago salado |
| Trips & Tours<br>Ausflüge & Touren | | Excursions & tours<br>Excursions & rutas |
| Perfect route<br>Perfekte Route | | Itinéraire idéal<br>Ruta perfecta |
| MARCO POLO Highlight | ⭐ | MARCO POLO Highlight |

# INDEX

This index lists all sights and destinations featured in this guide.
Numbers in bold indicate a main entry.

# CREDITS

# WRITE TO US

e-mail: info@marcopologuides.co.uk

Did you have a great holiday?
Is there something on your mind?
Whatever it is, let us know!
Whether you want to praise, alert us to errors or give us a personal tip – MARCO POLO would be pleased to hear from you.
We do everything we can to provide the very latest information for your trip.

Nevertheless, despite all of our authors' thorough research, errors can creep in. MARCO POLO does not accept any liability for this. Please contact us by e-mail or post.

MARCO POLO Travel Publishing Ltd
Pinewood, Chineham Business Park
Crockford Lane, Chineham
Basingstoke, Hampshire RG24 8AL
United Kingdom

**PICTURE CREDITS**
Cover photograph: Banff National Park, Laif: Harscher
U. Bernhart (3 bottom, 90/91, 94, 104/105); O. Bolch (12/13, 18/19, 39, 56, 112/113); © fotolia.com: flucas (17 top); DuMont Bildarchiv: Hicker (front flap left, front flap right, 2 top, 4, 5, 8, 9, 15, 21, 23, 29, 30 left, 30 right, 42, 44, 48, 61, 63, 65, 72, 85, 86, 92, 97, 107, 110, 113), Widmann (59); Getty Images: All Canada Photos (Wheatley) (3 centre, 80/81); G. Hartmann (75, 89, 119, 137); R. Hicker (36, 47, 114 bottom); Huber: Damm (10/11, 34), Huber (2 centre top, 24/25, 32/33, 108/109); © iStockphoto.com: arild andersen (17 bottom); Kitewing Sports Ltd.: Justin Bufton (16 centre); Laif: Don (112); Laif: Aurora (Shugar) (71), Harscher (1 top, 98/99), Heeb (2 bottom, 3 top, 50/51, 52, 66/67, 68, 124/125), hemis.fr (6), Hub (7, 27); H. Lange (111); mauritius images: Food and Drink (26 right), Foodpix (26 left, 28/29); T. Stankiewicz (28, 54, 57, 78, 82, 114 top, 115); K. Teuschl (2 centre bottom, 40/41, 76, 77, 101, 103); VAN DOP GALLERY: Trudy Van Dop (16 top); Vancouver Food Tour: Melody Fury (16 bottom)

**1st Edition 2014**
Worldwide Distribution: Marco Polo Travel Publishing Ltd, Pinewood, Chineham Business Park, Crockford Lane, Basingstoke, Hampshire RG24 8AL, United Kingdom. E-mail: sales@marcopolouk.com
© MAIRDUMONT GmbH & Co. KG, Ostfildern
Chief editor: Marion Zorn
Author: Karl Teuschl; editor: Marlis v. Hessert-Fraatz
Programme supervision: Anita Dahlinger, Ann-Katrin Kutzner, Nikolai Michaelis
Picture editors: Gabriele Forst, Barbara Schmid
What's hot: wunder media, Munich
Cartography road atlas & pull-out map: © MAIRDUMONT, Ostfildern
Design: milchhof : atelier, Berlin; Front cover, pull-out map cover, page 1: factor product munich
Translated from German by Wendy Barrow; editor of the English edition: Margaret Howie, fullproof.co.za
Prepress: M. Feuerstein, Wigel

# DOS & DON'TS ✊

**A few things you should bear in mind on your holiday**

## DO TRAVEL WITH HEALTH INSURANCE

As a foreigner you will be treated as a private patient and a day at a Canadian clinic can easily cost C$1000 and more. Ensure that you have foreign health insurance.

## DO SCARE OFF THE BEARS

Bears have an excellent sense of smell but have poor eyesight. If you are out walking upwind and surprise a bear they will be aggressive. When hiking it is best to talk loudly, sing or wear a bell on your leg so that you announce yourself and give any bears in the area time to move away.

## DON'T UNDERESTIMATE DISTANCES

Canada is a massive country and distances on the map can be deceiving. Especially in the vast north of the country where the width of a finger on the map can mean a very long day trip on seemingly endless dirt roads.

## DON'T GIVE THIEVES AN OPPORTUNITY

Canada is a very safe destination; however, it is always best not to give thieves an opportunity. So never leave cameras or other valuables in the car and at night avoid dark streets in the large cities.

## DON'T DRIVE UNDER THE INFLUENCE OF ALCOHOL

Although the limit is 0.8, in the event of an accident the insurance company will not pay out. In addition, the police show no mercy and the penalties are draconian.

## DO BE AWARE OF THE SMOKING LAWS

Smoking is frowned upon in Canada – and it is horrendously expensive. Smoking is prohibited in all public buildings, airports, and restaurants. Only in the furthest corner you might still find a smoking section.

## DO REMEMBER THE MOSQUITO REPELLENT

Do not go hiking without mosquito repellent in the Canadian bush – the mosquitoes will have a field day with you! A small bottle of *Off*, *Muskol* or *Cutter* will make all the difference.

## DO INFORM AUTHORITIES BEFORE SETTING OFF ON A HIKE

Whether it is just for a day, a week or an entire month that you plan for a hike or canoe trip: always leave a note with your hiking or canoeing route and the time of your return. Leave the information with canoe rentals, the bush pilots that take you into the hinterland, or with the wardens in the national parks.